THE FIVE GUARDIANS OF SPIRITUAL FERVOUR

PRESERVING OUR FIRST LOVE IN CHRIST

Yeshua S. Jehu

Yeshua S. Jehu

Appreciation

To God Almighty, who in His infinite grace has granted me divine revelations, timely resources, strengthening counsel, and unwavering guidance through every season. I give profound thanks for His abundant wisdom, faithfulness, and sovereign hand that has sustained, inspired, and carried this work from inception to completion. All glory belongs to Him alone.

Contents

THE FIVE GUARDIANS OF SPIRITUAL FERVOUR

Preface

Maintaining spiritual fervour is a struggle many believers face—especially those newly baptized in the Holy Spirit. The first flame burns bright, yet the heat can wane; zeal fades, and the heart that once burned for God can grow cold over time.

Troubled by this common dilemma and burdened for the Body of Christ, I sought the Lord in prayer for revelation: how does one avoid quenching the Spirit and continually mature in faith for the good of Christ's Bride?

The answer I received was not a single technique but five indispensable safeguards—five **Guardians** every believer must embrace. These Guardians protect against spiritual lethargy, cultivate steady growth, and preserve the fire God originally kindled within us. Thus was birthed *The Five Guardians of Spiritual Fervour.*

Be encouraged as you read and receive: your spirituality does not cancel your humanity — it perfects it. Spiritual life does not erase your human-ness; it refines and elevates it. This book will teach deep, revelatory spiritual truths, but the ultimate aim is practical: to make you a more faithful servant of God in the earth, useful for the salvation of lost souls and the advancement of God's will among men.

Introduction

A flourishing Christian life stands upon two non-negotiable disciplines: prayer and the study of the Word. These are not optional accessories or occasional exercises; they must become your lifestyle — the rhythm of your identity in Christ.

For this reason, prayer and the Word are not listed among the five Guardians as separate items. They are the foundation that undergirds every Guardian and every practice that follows. Absent daily communion with God and diligent engagement with Scripture, no method for sustaining fervour will succeed.

Communion with God — by prayer and by receiving His Word — is not duty alone but relationship. Cultivating a culture of constant communion forms a pattern of life that keeps you perpetually open to the movements of the Holy Spirit. The Spirit Himself is the true generator of fervour; prayer and Scripture are the means by which that life is maintained and empowered.

The five Guardians presented in this book are principles and practices that catalyze and sustain spiritual maturity. They are not isolated rules but integrated supports; each Guardian fortifies the others, creating a resilient chain of spiritual health. As Paul instructs: *"Never be lacking in zeal, but keep your spiritual fervour, serving the Lord."* (Romans 12:11, NIV.)

Fervour is more than transient emotion. It is a rooted, informed, grateful response to God's mercy that compels consistent spiritual investment. It strengthens the inner life and empowers one to walk in the Spirit, overcoming the flesh. *"Live by the Spirit, and you will not gratify the desires of the sinful nature."* (Galatians 5:16, NIV.)

Consecration to the Lord is the soil from which genuine spiritual vitality grows. Grace for fervour is required if consecration is to endure. Consecration aligns the believer with God's standards and preserves us from conforming to the world. As Paul exhorts: *"And do not be conformed to this world, but be transformed by the renewing of your mind, that you may prove what is that good and acceptable and perfect will of God."* (Romans 12:2, NKJV.)

Fervour births zeal. Where fervour is inwardly kindled, zeal—outward, energetic service—inevitably follows. The Scripture assures us that the sustained devotion of a righteous heart accomplishes much:

"The effective, fervent prayer of a righteous man avails much." (James 5:16, NKJV.) Jesus Himself embodied fervent devotion: *"During the days of Jesus' life on earth, He offered up prayers and petitions with loud cries and tears to the One who could save Him from death, and He was heard because of His reverent submission."* (Hebrews 5:7, NIV.)

While the words 'fervour' and 'zeal' are often used interchangeably, they carry distinct force. Zeal (Greek: *spoudē*, σπουδή) connotes earnestness, diligence, and active commitment—the visible labor of service. Fervour (Greek: *zeontes*, ζέοντες) literally means 'boiling' — a spiritual heat, an inward burning that animates and sustains outward action. Fervour produces zeal; the inward flame drives lasting outward fruit. When sustained, this dynamic produces works that outlast a single lifetime: *"A good man leaves an inheritance to his children's children."* (*Proverbs 13:22, NKJV.*)

In brief: zeal is energetic service; fervour is passionate devotion. Together they form the architecture of a truly alive Christian life.

The Five Guardians of Spiritual Fervour

The Guardians form an interconnected chain—each strengthening and upholding the others. They are not isolated principles but vital organs of one spiritual body. To lose one is to weaken the entire structure; to embrace them all is to produce spiritual resilience. These Guardians will empower every calling and project you undertake in the name of the Lord. Remember: fervour begets zeal; zeal produces fruit. When you do all things as unto the Lord, you will prosper spiritually and overcome the flesh's inclination to surrender.

We will now turn to the first Guardian, examining its scriptural foundation and its practical outworking. Through careful study and faithful practice, you will begin to see the flame of fervour not only ignited but maintained, carrying you deeper into the life for which God has called you.

THE FIRST GUARDIAN: PURPOSE

JUDGEMENT

Knowing and serving your purpose stands as the first Guardian of Spiritual Fervour because it answers the foundational question: **"Why?"** Purpose gives meaning to your labor, direction to your journey, and vision to your obedience. It prevents you from walking blindly or collapsing from discouragement due to lack of direction.

Purpose safeguards you from deception, drift, and stagnation. It anchors your pursuit, compelling your heart to rise above its present limits and reach toward the "more" that God has pre-appointed for you. In this way, purpose drives you deeper into consecration and into God Himself.

It is not that you will never feel overwhelmed or tempted to quit, but giving up means forfeiting the very meaning for which you were created. Therefore, you press on — because purpose keeps you pressing. Purpose supplies endurance, because you understand *why* you do what you do, and you are fueled by the fulfillment that comes from aligning with divine design.

Purpose compels consecration. It compels submission.

Under purpose, you must learn the discipline of submission. Serve those in spiritual authority over you, and the Lord Himself will promote you to higher ground. Value your spiritual leaders — honor them, serve them, love them — for through them, by the grace resting upon their lives, purpose will find you.

Just as in the parable of the talents, elevation comes only after the faithful servants fulfilled the purpose assigned to them. *(Matthew 25:14-30).* With purpose fulfilled, reward is credited to their account; and where reward appears, fervour is rekindled — motivation for more is protected from flickering.

For *whoever wants to be the greatest must become the servant of all.* (Matthew 20:26). Jesus affirmed that divine reward flows through honor and service:

"Anyone who receives a prophet because he is a prophet will receive a prophet's reward, and anyone who receives a righteous man because he is a righteous man will receive a righteous man's reward. And if anyone gives even a cup of cold water to one of these little ones because he is My disciple, I tell you the truth, he will certainly not lose his reward." (Matthew 10:41–42, NIV.)

Romans 8:28 establishes the foundation of this Guardian: *"And we know that all things work together for good to those who love God, to those who are the called according to His purpose."* (NKJV.) Purpose is therefore the comprehension of God's will for your life and the alignment of your strength, effort, and service with that design.

Work itself reflects purposeful design. Genesis reveals divine order in human vocation: *"Then the LORD God took the man and put him in the garden of Eden to tend and keep it."* (Genesis 2:15, NKJV.) You must take pride and delight in your labor. Scripture declares:

"I know that nothing is better for them than to rejoice, and to do good in their lives, and also that every man should eat and drink and enjoy the good of all his labor—it is the gift of God." (Ecclesiastes 3:12–13, NKJV.)

Work exists to keep man fruitful and forward-moving. Jesus affirmed this divine pattern: *"My Father is always at His work to this very day, and I, too, am working."* (John 5:17, NLT.) And Paul reveals the weight of this mystery—that our labor is not isolated from heaven but woven into the very mission of Christ: *"For we are God's fellow workers…"* (1 Corinthians 3:9, NKJV.)

This means every righteous task becomes a sacred partnership. You are not merely performing duties—you are advancing divine intention. Your effort becomes an offering, your diligence a spiritual weapon, your assignment a co-laboring with the King. When you grasp this truth, work ceases to feel mundane; it becomes ministry, stewardship, and worship.

God blesses the place of your assignment: For *"the LORD your God will bless you in all your produce and in all the work of your hands, so that you surely rejoice."* (Deuteronomy 16:15, NKJV.) Labor brings rest and satisfaction: *"The sleep of a laboring man is sweet, whether he eats little or much."* (Ecclesiastes 5:12, NKJV.)

Jesus echoed this principle: *"I have food to eat of which you do not know… My food is to do the will of Him who sent Me, and to finish His work."* (John 4:32, 34, NKJV.) Therefore, when you do God's will—serve purpose—you are nourished in ways human understanding cannot explain. You develop a peace that surpasses all human reasoning, and your spiritual fervour is guarded from flickering out. Purpose is nourishment; doing God's will sustains your fervour.

Psalm 16:11 summarizes the joy of walking purposefully with God; the pleasure you receive from it is what guards and sustains your spiritual fervour: *"You will show me the path of life; in Your presence is fullness of joy; at Your right hand are pleasures forevermore."* (NKJV.)

This joy is not emotional excitement but divine satisfaction. It is the delight that flows from walking in the path God ordained and experiencing the sweetness of His guiding presence. This is what sustains spiritual fervour.

But without purpose, the soul collapses. Anxiety intensifies, despair deepens, and fervour drains away. Therefore the psalmist cries: *"Teach me Your way, O LORD, and lead me in a smooth path, because of my enemies."* (Psalm 27:11, NKJV.)

Purpose cannot be sustained without discipline. God warns us not to resist His guidance: *"I will instruct you and teach you in the way you should go... Do not be like the horse or like the mule which have no understanding, which must be harnessed with bit and bridle, else they will not come near you."* (Psalm 32:8–9, NKJV.) A stubborn spirit loses purpose. A yielded spirit discovers destiny.

Jeremiah seals this truth: *"For I know the plans I have for you... plans for good and not for disaster, to give you a future and a hope."* (Jeremiah 29:11, NLT.)

Discovering Your Purpose

If you do not yet know your life's purpose — or if you know it but lack clarity — seek God deliberately. Two keys open this door:

1. **Counsel** — Surround yourself with wise, godly advisors who can perceive what you cannot, and learn how to hear the voice of God.

2. **Time and Dedication to Spiritual Growth** — Commit yourself to prayer, Scripture, worship, and quiet listening. Purpose is revealed to the spiritually mature and attentive.

Through counsel and consecrated pursuit, the Guardian of Purpose becomes established in your life, and your spiritual fervour is protected from every assault that seeks to extinguish your flame.

KEYS TO FINDING PURPOSE

<u>COUNSEL</u>

Counsel is the lifeline of purpose. It is the wisdom you do not yet possess but desperately need; it is the exterior insight that pierces your limitations and lifts you into clarity. Counsel is God sending illumination through voices, experiences, revelations, and ordained relationships so that the path of purpose becomes discernible. Without counsel, a man walks confidently yet blindly. Without counsel, zeal becomes reckless, fervour becomes unstable, and intention collapses under its own weight.

For **fervour without purpose is a chasing after the wind**—passion burning with no direction, energy expended with no eternal return. And

purpose without accurate counsel is a house built without foundation or defense—easily shaken, easily invaded, easily destroyed.

"Without counsel purposes are disappointed: but in the multitude of counsellors they are established." (Proverbs 15:22, KJV.)

Thus, it is your responsibility to intentionally position yourself where divine wisdom flows. Counsel must be pursued, honoured, and internalized. It is not enough to desire purpose; you must be shaped by truth, guided by wisdom, and anchored by revelation. *Enhancing your life with counsel is not optional—it is the bedrock of sustainable fervour and the guardrail that keeps your destiny from derailing.*

Learning to Hear God: The Primary Source

At the heart of discovering your purpose lies one unshakable truth: you must hear from the One who created you. God alone holds the blueprint of your life—the design, the timing, the path, the doors, the people, and the seasons. He alone knows the intricacies of your assignment, and He declares:

"For I know the plans I have for you... plans to prosper you and not to harm you, plans to give you a future and a hope." (Jeremiah 29:11, NIV)

To know your purpose, you must seek the One who authored it. Scripture commands: *"Ask and it will be given to you; seek and you will find; knock and the door will be opened to you."* (Matthew 7:7, NIV)

Seeking, asking, and knocking describe more than prayer—they describe a **relationship**. Purpose is not discovered through guesswork but through fellowship. It is born from communion with God, where your heart becomes familiar with His voice and sensitive to His leading.

Job reveals that God is never silent—only we are often inattentive: *"For God does speak—now one way, now another—though no one perceives it. In a dream, in a vision of the night..."* (Job 33:14–15, NIV)

God speaks continually, but perception requires spiritual discipline. A noisy soul cannot discern a divine whisper. A cluttered mind cannot sustain divine direction. Paul warns of what clouds perception: *"But I fear, lest somehow... your minds may be corrupted from the simplicity that is in Christ."* (2 Corinthians 11:3, NKJV)

False teachings, spiritual confusion, and overcomplicated doctrines contaminate clarity and distort God's voice. But the heart of God remains uncompromised: *"God... wants all people to be saved and to come to a knowledge of the truth."* (1 Timothy 2:3–4, NIV)

Jesus affirms this intimacy by saying: *"My sheep listen to my voice; I know them, and they follow me."* (John 10:27, NIV)

Therefore, finding purpose begins with cultivating spiritual hearing—through prayer, Scripture, quietness, obedience, and the humility that invites divine guidance. Purpose is not stumbled into; it is revealed through fellowship.

It is your sacred duty to ensure every avenue through which God speaks is functioning—your prayer life vibrant, your Scripture life consistent, your heart yielded. A believer who seeks purpose without a disciplined spiritual ear remains directionless.

Valuing the Graces in the Body of Christ

After God's direct counsel, He often uses His body—the church—to affirm, guide, sharpen, and activate your purpose. No believer is designed to journey alone. God distributes graces across His people, and these graces are meant to mature you, warn you, correct you, and launch you into your destiny.

Hebrews instructs: *"Obey your leaders and submit to their authority. They keep watch over you as men who must give an account. Obey them so that their work will be a joy, not a burden, for that will be of no advantage to you."* (Hebrews 13:17, NIV)

Spiritual leaders are entrusted with divine oversight. Their counsel provides safety; their correction provides stability; their guidance provides clarity. Submission to spiritual authority is not weakness—it is wisdom. It is the humility God honours and the posture through which He elevates.

Throughout Scripture, no one rose into divine purpose alone. Saul submitted to Samuel. David submitted to Samuel and Nathan. Barak submitted to Deborah. Elisha submitted to Elijah, and Timothy submitted to Paul.

Every destiny required alignment with spiritual leadership because purpose is always confirmed, strengthened, or activated through God's vessels.

Scripture also commands: *"Let us not give up meeting together... but let us encourage one another."* (Hebrews 10:25, NIV)

Community protects you from deception and isolation. Fellowship keeps you grounded in truth. Counsel, correction, encouragement, and accountability come through the community of faith—God's chosen environment for your growth.

Beware of false teachers whose corrupted doctrines contaminate destiny. Test every word by Scripture and by the Spirit. Surround yourself with wise counsellors—men and women who fear God, walk in truth, and steward His grace with purity.

When you honour spiritual counsel, submit to godly authority, and remain planted in a faithful community, you position yourself in the perfect environment to receive the clarity, refining, and defining needed to walk boldly in your God-ordained purpose.

TIME AND DEDICATION TO SPIRITUAL GROWTH

Time is always the determining factor of success and endurance. In time, everything is refined; in time, everything matures; in time, everything hidden is brought to light. Time is never still—its flow is constant, and when aligned with the will of God, it becomes one of your greatest allies. Through time, God shapes you, trains you, and expands you. Through the unfolding of seasons, He imparts knowledge, builds experience, and unveils the deeper layers of your purpose.

In the progression of time, new experiences refine us—sharpening our inner edge and producing new revelations, realisations, and holy adjustments that illuminate our calling with increasing clarity. Knowledge is received as the seasons pass; the spirit is fortified as time matures us. And when you remain dedicated to growing in spirit over the course of time, God entrusts you with more—more revelation, more responsibility, more grace. Your capacity enlarges as you progressively conform to His image and likeness. Only then does the fullness of your purpose stand before you in crystal clarity.

Scripture affirms this divine order of seasons: *"There is a time for everything, and a season for every activity under the heavens."* (Ecclesiastes 3:1, NIV)

Even the burdens and tensions of life operate on divine scheduling: *"For there is a proper time and procedure for every matter, though a person may be weighed down by misery."* (Ecclesiastes 8:6, NIV)

God Himself governs these seasons: *"He changes times and seasons; he deposes kings and raises up others. He gives wisdom to the wise and knowledge to the discerning."* (Daniel 2:21, NIV)

Time is not random; it is governed by His sovereign hand. Purpose unfolds only when the appointed season arrives, and Scripture reveals this truth with precision: *"When the fullness of time had come, God sent forth His Son..."* (Galatians 4:4, NKJV.)

The phrase *"the fullness of time"* tells us that purpose is never released prematurely. God waits for maturity, readiness, and alignment before unveiling destiny.

The apostle explains further: *"As long as the heir is a child, he is no different from a slave, although he owns the whole estate. He is subject to guardians and trustees until the time set by his father."* (Galatians 4:1–2, NIV). And again: *"So also, when we were children, were in slavery under the basic principles of the world. But when the time had fully come, God sent His Son..."* (Galatians 4:3–4, NIV).

This principle is unmistakable: before reaching maturity, you are like a child—possessing destiny in title but not yet capable of handling it in function. Destiny belongs to you, yet access is withheld until you can bear its weight.

The analogy is clear. A father may purchase a car for his child, but he will not allow an eight-year-old to drive it. Why? Because the child lacks maturity, judgment, and discipline. The car is valuable, and so is the child. To protect both the vehicle and the child, access is restricted until maturity is reached. It is a two-fold protection—preserving the child from self-inflicted harm and protecting the inheritance from misuse.

Likewise, God protects His divine purposes from immature believers. Spiritual infancy cannot steward spiritual inheritance. Immaturity collapses under responsibility; it mishandles calling; it misinterprets divine assignments. Therefore, God withholds certain doors, platforms, and revelations—not to deny you, but to preserve you.

This is why consecration, discipline, and immersion in the Word are indispensable. They build the internal stature necessary to carry divine purpose without breaking under its weight. **Maturity is the infrastructure of destiny.** God will not entrust you with deeper purposes until you are mature enough to sustain them.

Spiritual growth safeguards the believer and protects the integrity of God's plan. It strengthens the soul, sharpens discernment, and prepares the heart for the sacred trust of divine responsibility.

As Scripture declares the cry of the deep: *"Deep calls unto deep..."* (Psalm 42:7, NKJV)Your level of spiritual maturity determines the depth of revelation you can receive, the encounters you can withstand, and the assignments you can steward.

A lack of growth limits you. Peter exhorts: *"Like newborn babies, crave pure spiritual milk, so that by it you may grow up in your salvation."* (1 Peter 2:2, NIV)

Without spiritual growth, you remain vulnerable—easily deceived, easily overwhelmed, easily diverted from purpose. Stagnation stunts destiny. Immaturity delays promotion. Lack of development causes the believer to fall short of what God desires them to become—for their good, and for the fulfillment of His purposes.

To mature spiritually, you must intentionally and consistently feed your spirit with the Word, prayer, meditation, fellowship, and sound doctrine. These disciplines build stature and clarity. They define your boundaries, protect your freedoms, and illuminate your God-ordained purpose. In this maturity, you are propelled forward—confident, steadfast, and prepared to walk in the fullness of what God has designed for you.

Spiritual Maturity

Spiritual maturity is a fact that must never be overlooked by the church, for without it, there can be no mature stewardship of our divine inheritance and great commission in the world today. Only the mature can be entrusted to carry out the agenda of the Kingdom of God without the risk of folly and squander.

Paul instructs us: *"For by the grace given me I say to every one of you: Do not think of yourself more highly than you ought, but rather think of yourself with sober judgment, in accordance with the faith God has distributed to each of you."* (Romans 12:3, NIV)

Paul further exhorts believers to grow beyond the vulnerability of spiritual infancy: *"Then we will no longer be infants, tossed back and forth by the waves, and blown here and there by every wind of teaching and by the cunning and craftiness of men in their deceitful scheming."* (Ephesians 4:14, NIV)

Christian maturity is a journey from spiritual infancy (*nepios*) to mature sonship (*huios*), progressing through stages of growing understanding, application, responsibility, and strength in Christ. Maturity transforms one from a hearer of truth to a steward of truth—one capable of bearing weight, carrying assignment, and advancing the Kingdom without collapse.

Serving Purpose Causes Growth and Fervour

Purpose is the driving force behind spiritual growth and fervour. Purpose gives the answer to your 'why'. Why were you redeemed? Why were you created? Your God-ordained purpose is the answer.

Paul calls us to transformation instead of conformity: *"Do not conform to the pattern of this world, but be transformed by the renewing of your mind. Then you will be able to test and approve what God's will is—his good, pleasing and perfect will."* (Romans 12:2, NIV)

Acknowledging your need to serve God's purpose pushes you beyond limits, enabling you to do abundantly above what you ever thought possible. Purpose quickens the spirit. It commands alignment. It summons discipline.

Serving purpose motivates deeper prayer, more diligent reading of Scripture, and perseverance in the race of faith. Christ Himself exemplified purpose-driven living—unswayed by compromise, fixed on obedience, steadfast in fulfilling His divine calling. This propelled Him to rise early for prayer, retreat for communion, and endure the cross. It empowered Him to declare at the completion of His mission: *"It is finished."* (John 19:30)

Serving purpose breeds consecration. *"Be holy, for I am holy."* (1 Peter 1:16, NKJV). Holiness is not an accessory to purpose; it is embedded within it. The pursuit of God's purpose produces hunger for righteousness and a fervency fueled by the resolve not to fail in the assignment entrusted to you.

Purpose and holiness walk together. The purposes of God are saturated in righteousness. To walk in purpose is to contend for purity, because purpose demands consecration.

Discovering Your Life's Purpose and Ministry Calling

Discouragement is a scam of the enemy meant to deter you. Instead, let the recognition of your current unknowns excite and motivate you. Purpose discovery requires intentional action—one must prayerfully seek it and be diligent to pursue God's will concerning it. Then, one must prudently work in service of it to guard their spiritual fervour, *serving the Lord.*

"Never be lacking in zeal, but keep your spiritual fervour, serving the Lord." (Romans 12:11, NIV)

When you serve God by fulfilling your purpose, He rewards and encourages you, igniting fervour within. The fear of the Lord and devotion to purpose generate spiritual fervency and divine empowerment.

Purpose gives definition to, and a reason for existence. It restores and repairs your spiritual fervour and pushes you further into consecration so you may mature.

Testimonies—yours and those of others—serve as reminders of how God imparts purpose and transforms lives. As you serve purpose, you become increasingly aware of your insufficiency and more dependent on God. This dependency in turn fuels fervency: you pray deeper, search Scripture more diligently, and persevere with endurance because purpose anchors you.

Jesus modeled perfect purpose-living. Scripture affirms: *"I tell you the truth, the Son can do nothing by Himself; He can do only what He sees His Father doing, because whatever the Father does the Son also does."* (John 5:19, NIV)

For Christ, purpose was everything. It carried Him. It sustained Him. It empowered Him to endure, to focus, to finish—and ultimately to proclaim, *"It is finished."* (John 19:30)Purpose drove Him into early-morning prayer, into solitary communion, into constant preparation. Purpose trained Him, strengthened Him, and positioned Him to fulfil the will of the Father.

Purpose defines your very reason for living. It is the divine compass that directs your steps and anchors your existence in God's eternal will. For the Apostle Paul, purpose was the force that made him press on despite every circumstance.

In Philippians 1:21–26, he declares, *"For to me, to live is Christ and to die is gain. If I am to go on living in the body, this will mean fruitful labor for me. Yet what shall I choose? I do not know! I am torn between the two: I desire to depart and be with Christ, which is better by far; but it is more necessary for you that I remain in the body. Convinced of this, I know that I will remain, and I will continue with all of you for your progress and joy in the faith, so that through my being with you again your boasting in Christ Jesus will abound on account of me."*

Paul's purpose gave him reason to keep living, reason to keep pressing, reason to endure. His assignment to strengthen the churches—to help them grow and experience the joy of their faith—became the holy weight that compelled him forward. Purpose became his fuel, his resolve, and his sacred duty.

In conclusion: If you want to know your life's purpose or calling, go straight to the Author of life and purpose—God Himself: *Pray — Inquire of God;* Bold inquiry in prayer is the first step. God delights in revealing purpose to those who earnestly seek Him.

Consecrate Yourself to God; As you set yourself apart, God responds by unveiling deeper truths concerning your calling. Your level of consecration determines the measure of revelation God entrusts to you. Consecration is the visible sign of your willingness to be His co-worker in the kingdom. As you yield, God pours greater clarity and purpose into your life. Ownership invites investment—God reveals more to the surrendered.

These two pillars—prayer and consecration—are foundational. Consecration declares your eagerness to serve. Prayer unlocks the mysteries of your purpose. Together they position you to receive divine revelation.

As you engage with your purpose and serve God faithfully, He rewards you. His encouragement ignites and sustains spiritual fervour. The Parable of the Talents reaffirms this truth: God generously rewards diligence, stewardship, reverence, and wholehearted devotion. *(Matthew 25:14-30)*

Generators of Spiritual Fervour

As we delve further, it is important that we introduce the concept of 'generators of spiritual fervour.' These are truths, experiences, and profound understandings that rejuvenate spiritual vitality where it needs renewal. Hope and the fear of God are some examples of generators of the spiritual fervour necessary to serve God's purpose, and this fervour itself becomes a powerful guardian sustaining your spiritual vitality and growth. As we continue through the flow of the pages, more examples of other generators will be introduced and explained.

Hope as a Generator of Spiritual Fervour

Hope keeps the believer's vision forward-looking and anchored in God's promises. It fuels perseverance, endurance, and steadfastness—qualities essential for pursuing divine purpose despite obstacles. Scripture says, *"May the God of hope fill you with all joy and peace as you trust in him, so that you may overflow with hope by the power of the Holy Spirit."* (Romans 15:13, NIV).

This overflowing hope energizes the spirit, creating a fervency that propels continual service and consecration. Without hope, discouragement and weariness set in, diminishing fervour and weakening purpose.

Hope is the confident expectation of God's faithfulness and the fulfillment of His promises, including the realization of your God-ordained purpose. This confident expectation stirs your spirit, inspiring zeal and dedication that guard against spiritual lethargy. Without hope, there can be no true faith, for Scripture declares, *"Now faith is the substance of things hoped for, the evidence of things not seen."* (Hebrews 11:1, NKJV)

Hope births faith, and faith fuels fervour. Hope infuses the heart with divine anticipation, enabling you to continue serving God with passion while trusting His unfolding plan.

Fear of God as a Generator of Spiritual Fervour

The fear of God—understood as reverent awe and holy respect—instills a deep motivation to live righteously and serve faithfully. It anchors obedience and consecration, the vigorous commitment required for fulfilling purpose consistently.

Proverbs teaches, *"The fear of the LORD is the beginning of wisdom, and knowledge of the Holy One is understanding."* (Proverbs 9:10, NIV).

And again, *"The fear of the LORD leads to life; then one rests content, untouched by trouble."* (Proverbs 19:23, NIV).

This reverential fear generates spiritual fervour by stirring the believer's heart toward holiness and faithfulness. It ignites a passionate desire not to disappoint God or fail His cause—producing persistent zeal and obedient devotion.

Jesus commends such fervour linked to reverence and obedience, and the Parable of the Talents *(Matthew 25:14–30)* demonstrates that the right fear of God motivates faithful stewardship, which results in reward, promotion, and deeper responsibility. This creates a divine cycle that reinforces and elevates spiritual fervour.

How These Relate to Serving Purpose and Guarding Spiritual Fervour

Hope sustains your vision and commitment to purpose, while the fear of God motivates your holiness and faithful service. Together, they generate the fervour of spirit necessary not merely to initiate your divine purpose but to maintain it faithfully over the course of your life.

Serving purpose then becomes a guardian of spiritual fervour because your urgent focus and passion protect you from spiritual complacency, weariness, and distraction. Purpose-driven fervour safeguards your zeal, ensuring consistency in your walk, growth, and service to God.

In essence:

- Hope energizes your spirit with joy and expectancy.

- The fear of God anchors your dedication in reverence and obedience.

- This fervour fuels consecrated service to purpose.

- Serving purpose reinforces spiritual fervour, creating a protective cycle.

This dynamic interaction fortifies the believer in every season of the spiritual journey, enabling sustained growth, unwavering vitality, and enduring impact in God's kingdom.

THE SECOND GUARDIAN: STEADFASTNESS

JUDGEMENT

Steadfastness is a crucial guardian of spiritual fervour, embodying unwavering commitment, stability, and perseverance in the Christian walk. Defined as being fixed, unchanging, and unswerving, steadfastness leads believers to remain firm in faith and purpose regardless of life's trials and temptations. Steadfastness is spiritual strength—the ability to stand on the truth of the Word of God and the convictions of the Spirit of God, never departing from them.

A steadfast spirit is a spirit that can endure through the darkness of this world and remain pure, untainted, and anchored in the purity of Christ. A steadfast spirit is proof of spiritual maturity and the defining mark of spiritual strength. It is the steel required to stand against the forces of evil in this fallen world. Without steadfastness, your spiritual life is nothing but a grass-thatched house—lacking structural strength and devoid of a foundation that can support the weight of divine purpose.

Steadfastness is the strength for self-control, for without self-control you are defenseless, exposed, and spiritually vulnerable. Scripture warns: *"Whoever has no rule over his own spirit is like a city broken down, without walls."* (Proverbs 25:28, NKJV)

Steadfastness empowers you with a heart of patience—to stay strong, to believe, to endure, and to trust even when every odd seems to say otherwise concerning your faith. The Word affirms, *"But let patience have its perfect work, that you may be perfect and complete, lacking nothing."* (James 1:4, NKJV)And again, *"For you have need of endurance, so that after you have done the will of God, you may receive the promise."* (Hebrews 10:36, NKJV)

This is the inner architecture of steadfastness: the God-given strength to remain immovable in character, emotion, faith, and purpose.

2 Peter 3:17–18 (NKJV) declares: *"You therefore, beloved, since you know this beforehand, beware lest you also fall from your own steadfastness, being led away with the error of the wicked; but grow in the grace and knowledge of our Lord and Savior Jesus Christ..."*

You must know the truth to remain steadfast in it. When you have the Word of God as a lifestyle discipline—constantly shaping your convictions, calibrating your heart, and strengthening your faith—the power to stand upon its edifications with unwavering certainty is the essence of steadfastness.

Biblical Foundations and Meaning

1 Corinthians 15:58 exhorts believers: *"Therefore, my dear brothers and sisters, stand firm. Let nothing move you. Always give yourselves fully to the work of the Lord, because you know that your labor in the Lord is not in vain."* (NIV)

Steadfastness empowers you to give yourself fully to the work of the Lord, anchoring your soul in unwavering devotion and keeping you unmoved in your pursuit and divine endeavour.

The original Greek unveils the depth of steadfastness:

- **(hedraios)** — firm, immovable, grounded.

- **(kartereō)** — to endure with strength.

- **(hupomoné)** — steadfast patience and perseverance.

- **(statherótita)** — stability, unwavering consistency.

In Hebrew, steadfastness is captured in:

- **chesed** — steadfast love, covenant loyalty.

- **emunah** — faithfulness, firmness, dependability.

Summarizing the meaning of steadfastness:

Steadfastness is the spiritual architecture of immovability—rooted in covenant loyalty, sustained by endurance, expressed in faithful consistency, and empowered by the Spirit to remain fixed on truth regardless of pressure. It is loyalty in motion, endurance with conviction, and stability forged through revelation. It mirrors God's own steadfast nature, enabling the believer to reflect His unwavering faithfulness in their daily walk.

The Mindset of Steadfastness

Steadfastness means being level-headed and steady at all times, regardless of circumstances or emotions. Proverbs 24:10 warns, *"If you fail under pressure, your strength is too small."* (NLT)

And David pleads, *"Create in me a pure heart, O God, and renew a steadfast spirit within me."* (Psalm 51:10, NIV)

A steadfast spirit is thus the strength one requires to maintain purity, vitality, and the continued health of their spiritual life. Steadfastness of spirit becomes spiritual immunity—resisting the virus of sin, compromise, and weakness. It keeps the fervour of your intimacy with God strong, faithful, unwavering, and bolted to truth.

Your **mind-set** is the collection of internal settings governing how you perceive, behave, and respond. It is a spiritual bolt-system. When Scripture commands, *"Let this mind be in you which was also in Christ Jesus,"* (Philippians 2:5, NKJV) you must ask: *What structure formed the mind of Christ? Upon what settings was His mind bolted?* It was the **WORD OF GOD**—the eternal template of divine order.

To establish the mind of Christ within you, you must dwell richly and continually on the Word of God. 1 Timothy 4:8 (NLT) affirms, *"Physical training is good, but training for godliness is much better, promising benefits in this life and in the life to come."*

Dedication to physical improvement takes labor and discipline—how much more the cultivation of spiritual greatness? To attain both, one must balance their **kingly** *(responsibility, dominion)* and **priestly** *(consecration, intimacy)* duties. The path that builds the necessary inner strength to endure training, mature consistently, and continually ascend into Christlike stature is found in this guardian—**Steadfastness**.

Philippians 3:12–17 (NIV) reveals this determined pursuit. Paul writes, *"Not that I have already obtained all this... but I press on... forgetting what is behind and straining toward what is ahead... join with others in following my example..."*

Steadfastness is not passivity but holy aggression—active perseverance, unyielding devotion, and consistent labor in the Lord regardless of trials or discouragement.

2 Timothy 2:4 (NIV) anchors this: *"No one serving as a soldier gets entangled in civilian affairs, but rather tries to please his commanding officer."*

With steadfastness, the focus required to live above distraction is attained. You become unmoved by cultural pressures, unswayed by public opinion, and untouched by the menial expectations of society. Steadfastness empowers you to stand boldly in adversity, conflict, and persecution—holding to truth with unbreakable integrity and refusing compromise.

Philippians 3:14 declares, *"I press on toward the goal to win the prize for which God has called me heavenward in Christ Jesus."* (NIV)

How this 'pressing on' becomes the guardian of steadfastness:

Pressing on is the active expression of steadfastness. It is the spiritual propulsion required to pursue divine purpose against every odd and obstacle. It empowers you to reach toward God's desire for your life, to ascend toward the upward call of Christ, and to finish your divine assignment with excellence. Without steadfastness, pressing on becomes impossible, for only a steadfast spirit can carry the weight of purpose to completion.

Romans 12:12 reinforces this lifestyle: *"Rejoicing in hope, patient in tribulation, continuing steadfastly in prayer."* (NKJV)This is the culture of spiritual fervour made possible by steadfastness.

Finally, Scripture seals the mindset of this guardian: *"Let this mind be in you which was also in Christ Jesus."* (Philippians 2:5, NKJV)This verse encapsulates everything above—purity, discipline, endurance, unwavering devotion, and the unshakeable mind of Christ formed within the believer through steadfastness.

Steadfastness as a Safeguard in Spiritual Warfare

The spiritual battlefield remains ever-active; complacency is a silent killer. Pride and false security seduce believers into relaxing their vigilance, but steadfastness guards the soul against such spiritual negligence. Soldiers do not lay down their arms after a single victory—they remain alert for the duration of the war, discerning that though battles are won, the war itself continues. And our war is not against flesh and blood, but against powers, principalities, and rulers of darkness.

"For we do not wrestle against flesh and blood, but against principalities, against powers, against the rulers of the darkness of this age, against spiritual hosts of wickedness in the heavenly places." (Ephesians 6:12, NKJV)This war shall not end until Christ returns to crush the enemy underfoot. Until that glorious day, we remain vigilant with steadfast spirits and the sword of the Word of God held firm in hand.

The enemy's strategy is clear: to discourage your spiritual life and progress, to steal vitality, to kill momentum, and to destroy spiritual fervour. *"The thief does not come except to steal, and to kill, and to destroy." (John 10:10, NKJV)*

Believers are likened to sheep who understand the boundaries of their pasture yet remain vigilant against lurking wolves—never forgetting danger, never abandoning their posts.

"Be alert and of sober mind. Your enemy the devil prowls around like a roaring lion looking for someone to devour." (1 Peter 5:8, NIV)

Steadfastness maintains the believer's battle-readiness. It keeps the heart anchored, the mind sober, and the spiritual flame beyond the reach of demonic winds. It safeguards the zeal of the Spirit so the enemy cannot quench your fire nor undermine your devotion to God's work.

Do not forget the kingdom of darkness. Steadfastness protects you from complacency—from becoming smug and drowsy in the comfort of temporary success. Pride is the intoxication that blinds you to the enemy's continued advance. To relax fully, to turn your back, to leave your post—this is the doorway to defeat.

Humility, therefore, is the shield that guards your steadfastness. A humble spirit accepts correction. A humble heart welcomes rebuke. Humility is a seal of spiritual maturity—just as steadfastness is a tool of consecration. Meditation, too, remains a vital tool, sharpening vigilance and awakening spiritual sight.

Never forget: the warfare continues still. There is always a risk of losing a battle—this must never happen. The kingdom of darkness is always at work. Be diligent. Steadfastness is the key.

A wise warrior does not lower his guard simply because a battle is won. He discerns seasons: the time for war, the time for celebration, and the time for silence. A battle won is not proof that the war is over. In fact, the enemy often returns to the drawing board, strategizing their next strike. The battle belongs to the vigilant. The victory belongs to the prudent.

As a sheep knows the demarcations set by the Shepherd, it also remembers the image of the wolf. Its survival instinct remains sharp. It does not grow complacent amidst the freedom provided within the safety of the pasture. It remains conscious of predators hiding beyond the borders. It alerts the Shepherd. It protects the flock. It avoids the edges where danger lurks—walk not near the pitfalls of temptation.

Be conscious, therefore, that your enemy lurks with predatory intent. Keep vigilant. Keep your eyes open. Never turn your back lest he strike.

A soldier does not entangle himself in civilian affairs; he lives to please his Commander. Likewise, you must do the same. Victory in a battle does not mean victory in the war. The enemy may spring back. Do not allow him to win even one battle. You belong to a superior kingdom.

"The light shines in the darkness, and the darkness did not comprehend it." *(John 1:5, NKJV)* Be a good soldier. Keep your hand upon your weapon at all times. Our struggle is not earthly. Our enemies are not human. Our war is spiritual, invisible, ruthless.

The forces of darkness seek to drain believers of love for God, to deaden spiritual fervour, and to extinguish the fire of the Holy Spirit. Therefore—be diligent.

Steadfastness as a Mark of Spiritual Maturity

Psalm 131 exalts the soul that has matured beyond childish impulses:

"My heart is not proud, LORD, my eyes are not haughty; I do not concern myself with great matters or things too wonderful for me. But I have calmed and quieted myself, I am like a weaned child with its mother; like a weaned child I am content." (Psalm 131:1–2, NIV)

Such maturity is marked by trust, contentment, peace, and emotional stillness. Steadfastness weans you off the impulses of spiritual infancy. For with maturity comes discernment—knowing what drains your spiritual vitality and what strengthens your inner man.

"You will keep in perfect peace him whose mind is steadfast, because he trusts in You." (Isaiah 26:3, NIV)

Faith in God generates spiritual fervour; it intensifies the engine of steadfastness. When your trust is fixed on Him, He keeps you in perfect peace—your mind fortified, your emotions anchored.

Philippians 4:6–7 calls believers into this matured posture: *"Do not be anxious about anything, but in everything, by prayer and petition, with thanksgiving, present your requests to God. And the peace of God, which transcends all understanding, will guard your hearts and your minds in Christ Jesus." (NIV)*

Paul's personal testimony reveals a life schooled in steadfast endurance: *"I have learned in whatever state I am, to be content. I know how to be abased, and I know how to abound. Everywhere and in all things I have learned both to be full and to be hungry, both to abound and to suffer need." (Philippians 4:11–12, NKJV)*

Contentment is not innate—it is learned. It is matured into. It is the fruit of a steadfast spirit. *"But godliness with contentment is great gain." (1 Timothy 6:6, NIV)*

Contentment is the posture of a matured warrior who no longer craves the excesses that weaken the spirit. Steadfastness trains you into this maturity. It disciplines your desires. It steadies your journey. It elevates you to higher planes of spiritual stature. *(2Corinthians 4:17-18).*

Practical Wisdom and Cautions: Indicators of a Steadfast Spirit

If you manifest the following, you have the basic indicators and essence of a mature steadfast spirit—the right mentality of spiritual maturity to foster your walk with God.

Control Emotions: High emotions, even righteous anger, can cloud judgment. *"Do not be quickly provoked in your spirit, for anger resides in the lap of fools."* (Ecclesiastes 7:9, NIV)

Decisions should never be made solely under emotional influence. Steadfastness says: ***Beware of over-excitement. Discouragement is a scam. Frustration is a scam.***

These are disciplines learned through the principles of the five guardians of spiritual fervour. Every decision influenced by emotions should be subjected to a second opinion—one not biased before its establishment. Only a mind rich in truth and bolted down by steadfastness in the wisdom thereof can function with such prudence.

"Don't sin by letting anger control you. Think about it overnight and remain silent." (Psalm 4:4, NLT). Don't allow highs to throw you off. Be steadfast—steady and fastened. Neither allow lows to throw you off the mark. Remain steady and fastened to the vision, to purpose, and to serving it.

Exercise Patience: True quality work comes from detailed attention and disciplined patience, a consistency that is characteristic of a steadfast spirit.. Speed without patience breeds frustration and subpar outcomes. Do not neglect perfection by doing your work carelessly or in a rushing manner—no matter who or what compels you, even if it is you.

Understand that perception causes reception and that first impressions seal the deal. Be keen to detail. You may accidentally lead those you are supposed to minister to away because of an accidentally placed action or distortion of image responsible for reputation in your work. With everything you do, keep in mind that you aren't working for yourself alone but for the body of Christ. We are interdependent.

It is attention to detail that births quality. Patience is a virtue. Speed is a product of mastery of your discipline. Frustration is birthed when speed goes ahead of patience, which leads to the eventual lack of quality and self-assertion in the work of your hands. It also leads to rejection because quality trumps speed. The King's work is indeed promptly attended to, yet it is attended to cautiously, with attention to detail.

The problem with most of us is we want speed without the virtue of patience. Mansions aren't built in a day. And even if some are built faster than others, there is still meticulous attention to detail from the foundation up.

Guard Your Tongue: Silence can be a sign of wisdom and trustworthiness, inviting greater responsibilities in God's kingdom. Silence, too, is a sign of a steadfast spirit. To know when to speak and when to prudently hold back—holy discretion for divine purposes—only with steadfastness of spirit can you protect the agenda of God from premature exposure, and only with a steadfast spirit can you carry out your divine purpose unswervingly.

Beware peak vulnerability: Spiritual peaks often precede falls if vigilance lapses. This is where steadfastness guards you. Glorify God, not your power or gifts, maintaining a steady focus on His purpose. This is proof of steadfastness.

"My heart is not proud, LORD, my eyes are not haughty; I do not concern myself with great matters or things too wonderful for me. But I have calmed and quieted myself...Israel, put your hope in the LORD both now and forevermore." (Psalm 131:1–3, NIV)

Understand that when you peak, you fall—that is when you are most vulnerable. You will always fall unless you deliberately refuse to give preeminence to the peak and instead focus your attention and thanksgiving on the God who facilitated the peak.

Don't make a big deal of anything. It's not the focus. The power made manifest is not the focus. It's God. It's Christ. It's His Word and maintaining a relationship with Him.

You should be tense as an injured lioness every time you are at peak—so as not to give the enemy a chance. Elijah called down fire from heaven and it happened, yet he did not give it preeminence. Paul raised a man from the dead after he fell from a third-story window, yet he simply continued preaching. It didn't phase him, for it is not the focus.

The ways of God are the focus—not the deeds. The deeds simply attract men to the kingdom. Never let these things get to you. They are too petty to dwell on. Forget them, for God is always doing a new thing—even the greatest miracle is not the focus.

Christ walked on water, raised the dead, multiplied food, turned water into wine—yet He never gave these things preeminence. They were simply for people to see and be drawn to the Word. They grant credibility. *"If I be a man of God…"* (2 Kings 1:12)

Understand the danger and vulnerability in peaking if you give it preeminence—like David did, and the sin with Bathsheba happened. Understand that when you place confidence in peaks, ***"when you peak, you will most definitely fall if not on your guard."***

"If you think you are standing strong, be careful not to fall. The temptations in your life are no different from what others experience. And God is faithful… When you are tempted, he will show you a way out so that you can endure." (1 Corinthians 10:12–13, NLT)

Verses like 2 Peter 3:17–18 exhort believers to guard their steadfastness while growing in grace and knowledge. *"Therefore, dear friends… be on your guard so that you may not be carried away… and fall from your secure position. But grow in the grace and knowledge of our Lord and Savior Jesus Christ."* (NIV)

The race set before us calls for endurance and unswerving loyalty: *"…let us run with endurance the race God has set before us."* (Hebrews 12:1, NLT)

Steadfastness is the firm foundation on which spiritual fervour is sustained. It keeps us anchored, vigilant, and faithful—constantly engaged in God's work and protected against the enemy's advances.

By cultivating steadfastness, believers embody true maturity and empower their spiritual fervour to flourish as a guarding force in their Christian journey.

"Preach the word; be prepared in season and out of season; correct, rebuke and encourage—with great patience and careful instruction." (2 Timothy 4:2, NIV) This is an example of being steadfast—the sheer consistency and diligence. Such is the maturity of a steadfast spirit.

HOW TO CULTIVATE A HEART OF STEADFASTNESS

GENERATORS OF SPIRITUAL FERVOUR

The Fear of God: True reverence and awe for God is the only legitimate fear; all other fears are forms of idolatry that distract and enslave the soul.

"The Lord Almighty is the one you are to regard as holy, He is the one you are to fear, He is the one you are to dread. He will be a holy place…" (Isaiah 8:13–14, NIV)

Here, the fear of God is tied directly to reverence and trust as our only safety and hope, warning against fear born from people or distrusting God. This sacred fear nurtures steadfastness by grounding the heart in holy dependence.

To walk steadfastly, cultivate a heart of contentment. Whether in abundance or scarcity, fix your joy and satisfaction in the Lord alone. Materialism and the wrong motivations in pursuit of earthly wealth threaten spiritual fervour and steadfastness:

"It is easier for a camel to go through the eye of a needle than for someone who is rich to enter the kingdom of God." (Mark 10:25, NIV)

While God blesses His children with material prosperity, centering your heart on these blessings leads to dissatisfaction and vulnerability. Instead, store treasures in heaven:

"Do not store up for yourselves treasures on earth... But store up for yourselves treasures in heaven." (Matthew 6:19–20, NIV)

"Command those who are rich... not to be arrogant nor to put their hope in wealth, which is so uncertain, but to put their hope in God." (1 Timothy 6:17, NIV)

Remaining steadfast in the truth of the Word concerning how we should live protects us from arrogance and preserves the sweetness of spiritual fervour.

Let your heart be anchored in eternal riches. When blessings increase, your steadfastness remains unshaken because your true wealth is found in God. Your spirit will not waver, and your focus will remain unswerving on what genuinely matters—God.

Steadfastness is both a mark and a powerful tool of spiritual maturity, shaping believers into unwavering vessels of God's glory and purpose. *"By your steadfastness and patient endurance you shall win the true life of your souls."* (Luke 21:19, AMP)

THE THIRD GUARDIAN: HUMILITY

JUDGEMENT

Humility is the very nature of God and the essence He calls us to embody. Scripture teaches that *"God resists the proud but gives grace to the humble."* (James 4:6). Those who are humble receive God's blessing, for they walk in the Spirit's favor and protection. This divine posture counters the natural human instinct for exaltation, which is the root of pride and downfall.

Many great servants of God have fallen because they neglected the small seeds of pride that crept into their hearts, seeds watered by demonic subtlety to lead them astray. There is no room for boasting in anything but the Lord alone. As Paul declares in 1 Corinthians 1:31, *"Let him who boasts boast in the Lord."* (NIV)

This is because none of the gifts or blessings we receive from the Holy Spirit are earned by our own effort—as we see *1 Corinthians 1:26-29* explain—God uses what the world considers foolish and weak precisely to nullify human boasting.

Paul further warns, *"Do not deceive yourselves. If any of you think you are wise by the standards of this age, you should become 'fools' so that you may become wise."* (1 Corinthians 3:18, NIV). Human wisdom is folly before God, for *"He catches the wise in their craftiness."* (1 Corinthians 3:19).

The wisdom we receive as Spirit-filled believers is a divine gift, freely given for God's glory alone, never to be claimed as our own. Isaiah 42:8 underscores God's exclusive glory: *"I am the LORD; that is My name; and My glory I will not give to another, nor My praise to carved images."* (NKJV)

Foundations of Humility as a Guardian of Spiritual Fervour

Romans 12:16 admonishes us, *"Live in harmony with one another. Do not be proud, but be willing to associate with people of low position. Do not be conceited."* (NIV) Conceit is simply believing you know it all, which blocks growth and unity. Likewise, Romans 12:3 reminds us, *"Do not think of yourself more highly than you ought, but rather think of yourself with sober judgment..."* (NIV).

The wisdom of humility resonates through Proverbs: *"He mocks proud mockers but shows favor to the humble and oppressed."* (Proverbs 3:34, NI V). *"The LORD hates... A proud look."* (Proverbs 6:16-17, NKJV)

"Trust in the LORD with all your heart; do not depend on your own understanding. Seek his will in all you do, and he will show you which path to take." (Proverbs 3:5-6, NLT)

"Do not be wise in your own eyes; fear the Lord and shun evil. This will bring health to your body and nourishment to your bones." (Proverbs 3:7-8, NIV)

Humility invites correction: *"My child, do not despise the LORD's discipline, and do not resent His rebuke."* (Proverbs 3:11-12, NIV). Being humble enough to accept rebuke is a profound sign of maturity and a key tool in consecration. Further, *Proverbs 9:7-9* explains that the wise welcome correction and grow wiser, while the proud reject it and invite harm.

Proverbs 10:17 tells us, *"People who accept discipline are on the pathway to life, but those who ignore correction will go astray."* (NLT) *"Pride leads to disgrace, but with humility comes wisdom."* (Proverbs 11:2, NLT)

"A gentle answer turns away wrath, but harsh words stir up anger." (Proverbs 15:1, NIV) *"Humility and the fear of the Lord bring wealth and honor and life."* (Proverbs 22:4, NIV)

"Pride ends in humiliation, while humility brings honor." (Proverbs 29:23, NIV) Together, these scriptures unfold humility as the heart posture that sustains spiritual fervour by fostering teachability, unity, and reverence for God.

The Power of the Body of Christ: Interdependence and Unity

Humility also leads us to embrace the power of the body of Christ. No one operates in isolation; no great work is accomplished alone. The spiritual victories and divine manifestations that a servant of God attains are the fruit of intercessory prayer, the faithfulness of those who give, and the blessings touching entire families. The grace upon any individual is the cumulative result of cooperation within the body of Christ. Whether conscious of it or not, no believer is saved or empowered without the spiritual teamwork of the church.

Therefore, it is essential to build the right relationships—fellowship with those who desire your prosperity, who pray for you, and who support your God-ordained journey as you yourself remain humble enough to do the same for them. God has ordained this divine network of graces as a solution to your struggles.

If you reject or neglect the graces and leaders around you, you reject the very means God has provided for your growth and breakthrough. God's promises are 'yes and amen' through Christ Jesus, *2 Corinthians 1:20*; all spiritual resources in the heavenly realms are at your disposal.

2 Peter 1:3— *"His divine power has given us everything we need for a godly life through our knowledge of him who called us by his own glory and goodness."* (NIV) Take full advantage of these divine provisions by humbly aligning yourself with the body of Christ. Humility is key to unlocking and sustaining these blessings.

Humility is the very nature of God and the essence He requires from His followers. Scripture reveals that God *"resists the proud but gives grace to the humble,"* (James 4:6, NKJV; also 1 Peter 5:5) underscoring humility as not only a divine attribute but also a prerequisite for receiving God's favor. Blessed indeed are the humble, for they are positioned to walk in spiritual strength and vitality.

This divine nature stands in stark contrast to humanity's innate craving for exaltation and pride—a poison that has led many to fall because they neglected the subtle beginnings of their pride. The only boast we have is in the God. Spiritual gifts and blessings are freely given by grace; they are not earned, and thus no human may proudly claim them as their own *(1 Corinthians 1:26-29).*

The wisdom granted to Spirit-filled believers is a gift to be used for God's glory, not for personal exaltation. God alone holds the glory: *(Isaiah 42: 8).* Humility is not timidity. It is a controlled and active strength. Have the humility of the Lord, for He can only use the humble.

THEMES OF HUMILITY

Humility That Comes from Wisdom

James 3:13 teaches, *"Who is wise and understanding among you? Let him show it by his good life, by deeds done in the humility that comes from wisdom."* (NIV) True wisdom manifests itself in humility—a purity of spirit that is peace-loving, considerate, submissive, merciful, impartial, and sincere *(James 3:16–17).* Such humility honours God and guards spiritual fervour. Jesus extends a blessing to the peacemakers—those who embody humility and foster peace—calling them *"sons of God"* *(Matthew 5:9, NKJV).*

Colossians 4:5–6 invites believers to live wisely and speak graciously, illustrating humility as practical wisdom in interaction with others. *"Walk in wisdom toward those who are outside, redeeming the time. Let your speech always be with grace, seasoned with salt, that you may know how you ought to answer each one."* (NIV). This is humility in action: considerate, patient, and filled with grace.

The Apostle Paul: A Pattern of Humility

Paul exemplifies humility in both his conduct and teachings. Addressing the Corinthian church, he defends his ministry saying, *"You have made me act like a fool. You ought to be writing commendations for me, for I am not at all inferior to these 'super apostles,' even though I am nothing at all"*

(2 Corinthians 12:11, NLT). Rather than self-promotion, Paul lets God's work through him commend him *"When people commend themselves, it doesn't count for much. The important thing is for the Lord to commend them."* (2 Corinthians 10:18, NLT).

Paul's Reference to Being "Caught Up to the Third Heaven"

This occurs in 2 Corinthians 12:2–7, where Paul describes a profound spiritual experience. He uses the phrase *"I know a man in Christ"* to speak about himself. This choice of words has led to significant interpretation and analysis. Let us read it in the ***New International version***, then explain further.

2 Corinthians 12:1–7 (NIV)

"I must go on boasting. Although there is nothing to be gained, I will go on to visions and revelations from the Lord. I know a man in Christ who fourteen years ago was caught up to the third heaven. Whether it was in the body or out of the body I do not know—God knows. And I know that this man—whether in the body or apart from the body I do not know, but God knows—was caught up to paradise and heard inexpressible things, things that no one is permitted to tell.

I will boast about a man like that, but I will not boast about myself, except about my weaknesses. Even if I should choose to boast, I would not be a fool, because I would be speaking the truth. But I refrain, so no one will think more of me than is warranted by what I do or say, or because of these surpassingly great revelations. Therefore, in order to keep me from becoming conceited, I was given a thorn in my flesh, a messenger of Satan, to torment me."

Paul spoke in third person in this portion of his second epistle to the Corinthian church as a show of humility. Paul is indeed referring to himself in this passage. Although he speaks in the third person, this rhetorical choice serves as a means of humility and to avoid the appearance of boasting.

He mentions that this experience occurred fourteen years prior, likely during a time when he was stoned and left for dead in Lystra *(Acts 14:19–20)*, suggesting it was a significant encounter with God. By using third-person language, Paul distances himself from direct self-promotion, which aligns with his broader message of humility throughout his letters.

Why Use Third-Person Language?

Paul's choice to describe his experience in the third person can be understood as an effort to emphasize humility. He aims to convey that the revelations he received were not for personal glory but rather as part of his apostolic authority.

This method of speaking about oneself indirectly was common in ancient rhetoric, especially when addressing sensitive topics like personal experiences of divine revelation. Paul was aware that his readers would understand the context he was using and that they would learn from his tactic a nugget of wisdom on how to maintain humility in the place of peak experiences.

Furthermore, he expresses concern about pride due to these revelations, mentioning a *'thorn in the flesh'* given to him to prevent him from becoming conceited. This is a powerful example of humility stemming from a place of true wisdom which is considerate. Paul understood that he was a role model and was supposed to teach these people by being a true pattern man of humility. He chose to use this as a teaching moment even as he defended his authority against the false teachers that refuted it.

He simultaneously gave them a nugget of wisdom in how to remain humble even whilst testifying about experiences that may bring praise to a man. He showed the people how to communicate such great personal experiences in Christ whilst simultaneously evading the possibility of being praised by man and ultimately directing their praise to the rightful person—our LORD and Saviour Jesus Christ. Paul's humility here is so great it is abounding in wisdom!

Paul's use of third-person language when describing his transcendental experience is a conscious act of humility, avoiding personal glorification and directing praise exclusively to God. This rhetorical choice offers believers profound wisdom on remaining humble even amid spiritual highs and revelations.

Humility That Stems from Love

Love is a character of people of humility. When you love, you lay down your life. You cease to have an ego. You lower yourself because of love. You come low for the benefit of another.

True humility originates from a heart of love. Love literally lays down life, lowering self-interest for the benefit of others. Jesus teaches this in Matthew 20:26–28, *"Whoever wants to become great among you must be your servant, and whoever wants to be first must be your slave—just as the Son of Man did not come to be served, but to serve, and to give his life as a ransom for many."* (NIV). By this, He was emphasizing servant leadership and self-sacrifice, underscored by His own example in washing His disciples' feet *(John 13:12–17).*

Genuine humility reveals itself in loving deeds, in choosing good over retaliation, even amidst hostility. Love fuels spiritual vitality and sustains fervour even in the darkest times. It is one of the generators of spiritual fervour.

True humility is sourced from a place of love. Where there is no love, there is no humility. The labors of love beget humility. It is the sacrifices done in love that truly reveal a humble spirit within a person. Even in a place of hostility, if a person chooses to show love—to repay evil for good—that is an expression of humility from a heart overwhelmed with the love of God. Love is a generator of spiritual vitality. Even in the darkest of circumstances, your spirit is not discouraged but continues to function unswervingly in the way God desires.

The Humility of Christ: Our Model

Christ's humility is the ultimate example. Though fully God—*"in Him dwells all the fullness of the Godhead bodily"* (Colossians 2:9, NKJV)—He chose the humble position of a servant, taking on human frailty and dying a criminal's death on the cross *(Philippians 2:5–8).*

His incarnation and sacrifice exemplify divine humility compelled by love; though rich, He became poor for our sake *(2 Corinthians 8:9).* Yet God exalted Him to the highest place, giving Him the name above all names *(Philippians 2:9–11).*

This principle is clear: *"whoever exalts himself will be humbled, and he who humbles himself will be exalted."* (Matthew 23:12, NKJV).Humility invites God's lifting, believers should clothe themselves in humility, for God opposes the proud but gives grace to the humble.

***The humility of Christ compelled by love is what that led to our
salvation***

Let us begin with describing who Christ truly is, to open up your mind
to see the magnitude of His humble sacrifice for us. Let us read from
Colossians 2:9–10 and *Colossians 1:15–20.*

Colossians 2:9–10 (NKJV)

*"For in Him dwells all the fullness of the Godhead bodily; and you are
complete in Him, who is the head of all principality and power."*

The 'fullness of God'—Creator of Heaven and earth—dwelt, dwells, and
shall forevermore dwell in Christ, for Christ Himself is God in bodily
form. Let us continue;

Colossians 1:15–20 (NKJV)

*"He is the image of the invisible God, the firstborn over all creation. For by
Him all things were created that are in heaven and that are on earth, visible
and invisible, whether thrones or dominions or principalities or powers. All
things were created through Him and for Him. And He is before all things,
and in Him all things consist. And He is the head of the body, the church,
who is the beginning, the firstborn from the dead, that in all things He may
have the preeminence."*

The Attitude of Christ

Philippians 2:5–8 (NLT)

*"You must have the same attitude that Christ Jesus had. Though he was God,
he did not think of equality with God as something to cling to. Instead, he
gave up his divine privileges; he took the humble position of a slave and was*

born as a human being. When he appeared in human form, he humbled himself in obedience to God and died a criminal's death on a cross."

This attitude of Christ is an attitude of true humility compelled by love. He emptied Himself of His 'Godness' for our sake. He left the streets of gold to walk the dusty streets of Jerusalem just so we may be reconciled to God and receive salvation through Him. *(John 3:16)*. He became poor for our sake so we may through Him become rich *(2 Corinthians 8:9)*. He became a humble servant—though He was God—just so He could save our souls from destruction.

Though owning the cattle on a thousand hills, *(Psalms 50:10)*, He chose to be born in a manger and into a poor family. Though immortal, He made Himself mortal and humbled Himself to a humiliating death on a cross so we could be reconciled to God and receive new life in Him through His resurrection.

This is ***TRUE HUMILITY. WITHOUT LOVE, THERE CAN BE NO HUMILITY!***

God demonstrated true humility. We are called to be imitators of Christ. We are called to grow into the fullness of Christ *(Ephesians 4:13)*. Follow His example and learn true humility.

Because of this, God exalted Christ:

Philippians 2:9–11 (NKJV)

"Therefore God also has highly exalted Him and given Him the name which is above every name, that at the name of Jesus every knee should bow, of those in heaven, and of those on earth, and of those under the earth, and that every tongue should confess that Jesus Christ is Lord, to the glory of God the Father."

This is a principle that will reward you and guard your spiritual vitality in God. Only through humility will God truly reward you: *"But those who exalt themselves will be humbled, and those who humble themselves will be exalted."* (Matthew 23:12, NLT)

"In the same way, you who are younger must accept the authority of the elders. And all of you, dress yourselves in humility as you relate to one another, for "God opposes the proud but gives grace to the humble." So humble yourselves under the mighty power of God, and at the right time he will lift you up in honor. (1 Peter 5:5–6, NLT)

A Final Charge on Humility

Pride precedes a fall, and great men of God have fallen through neglecting early signs of pride's growth. There is no place for boasting except in the Lord *(1 Corinthians 1:26–29)*. We must embrace God's wisdom, which often appears foolish to the world *(1 Corinthians 3:18–19)*. The glory belongs to God alone *(Isaiah 42:8)*.

Humility is power under control. God, the Almighty, demonstrated awe-inspiring humility by becoming like us, bearing our sins, and offering Himself as Savior. He seeks entry into hearts through invitation, not force—a model for us to follow. He made Himself in every way like us, bore our infirmity, and delivered us through His death on the cross and resurrection. Though possessing all authority, He chooses to knock gently; He does not force His entry but grants us free will. This is the humility of God.

The Holy Spirit—fully possessing the power of God—chooses to manifest as a gentle dove and speak in a still small voice. God Almighty chose not to exercise His power in judgment over the entire world but chose to love it instead. He humbled Himself and sent His only begotten Son, Christ Jesus, to die for our sins, that whosoever believes in Him shall not perish but have eternal life. God's love and humility define our example and calling.

You cannot serve God without humility. 'Be holy, for God am holy.' We are to emulate Christ. Christ's life was a model of humility. God resists the proud but exalts the humble. Only by following Christ's humble example will we grow into His fullness and maintain a fervent, fruitful spiritual life.

THE FOURTH GUARDIAN: WORSHIP

JUDGEMENT

Worship can be described as a heartfelt response of reverence, devotion, and adoration stirred by God's actions, His being, His presence, and His promises. Worship is rooted in depth and intended to be intimate. From worship flows rejuvenation—an experience in which the human spirit tastes divine pleasure, receives healing, and finds restoration. Worship repairs broken hearts, heals wounded souls, and creates an atmosphere of deep love and adoration for the goodness of God.

Worship is so profound that God created sex to typify it. Sex is a physical representation of spiritual intimacy—designed by God to give humanity a basic understanding of the depths of worship in the Spirit. Marriage itself was created as a sanctuary where God dwells.

"Judah has been unfaithful. A detestable thing has been committed in Israel and in Jerusalem: Judah has desecrated the sanctuary the LORD loves by marrying women who worship a foreign god... Has not the one God made you? You belong to him in body and spirit. And what does the one God seek? Godly offspring. So be on your guard, and do not be unfaithful to the wife of your youth."— (Malachi 2:11–15, NIV)

The sanctuary the LORD loves is marriage, and a sanctuary is a *place of worship.* Therefore, the deep union of husband and wife in the marriage bed is a divine typification—offering a glimpse into the profound intimacy of true spiritual worship. From such depth flows renewed fervour, fresh affection, and a revived adoration for God. ***This is the heart of worship.***

TRUE WORSHIP

True worship cannot occur without the Spirit of God. The union of husband and wife in marriage symbolizes the very intimacy worship demands—a depth of spiritual connection. To remain aligned with the heart of worship, we must walk in step with the Spirit and guard ourselves from the decline of the Church of Ephesus. Christ spoke to them saying:

"But I have this complaint against you. You don't love Me or each other as you did at first! Look how far you have fallen! Turn back to Me and do the works you did at first. If you don't repent, I will come and remove your lampstand from its place among the churches."— (Revelation 2:4–5, NLT)

This warning reveals the necessity of returning to genuine worship—marked by love, devotion, and spiritual intimacy.

Jesus further revealed the nature of true worship in His conversation with the Samaritan woman: *"But the hour is coming, and now is, when the true worshipers will worship the Father in spirit and truth; for the Father is seeking such to worship Him. God is Spirit, and those who worship Him must worship in spirit and truth."*— (John 4:23–24, NKJV)

True worship transcends location and ritual. It flows from a heart yielded to God and a spirit aligned with truth.

The Apostle Paul urges believers: *"I beseech you therefore, brethren, by the mercies of God, that you present your bodies a living sacrifice, holy, acceptable to God, which is your reasonable service."*— (Romans 12:1, NKJV)

Worship, therefore, is our spiritual service—our whole being offered as a living sacrifice.

Paul further clarifies: *"For we are the circumcision, who worship God in the Spirit, rejoice in Christ Jesus, and have no confidence in the flesh."*— (Philippians 3:3, NKJV)

True worship arises from spiritual transformation—not empty rituals, not fleshly confidence, but a heart engaged with God.

That secret thing that keeps you loving God—your remembrance of where He brought you from, the gospel, the sacrifice of Christ, the blood He shed for you *(John 3:16)*—this must be the core of your worship. Your personal reason for loving God may include His calling on your life or the countless blessings He has given you. Whatever it is, nurture it. ***Cultivate the generator of genuine love and adoration for God. From that place alone can true worship flow.***

Worship refills your cup with oil. When you worship, the LORD replenishes and reenergizes you. This rejuvenation preserves your steadiness in spiritual fervour—making worship an essential guardian of Spiritual Fervour.

EXPRESSIONS OF WORSHIP

Make it a daily custom to interact with the many demonstrations of worship. Worship is a deep and profound essence every believer must cultivate into their lifestyle. Its expressions are many, and the field is vast—overflowing with opportunities to learn, grow, and ascend spiritually. The KING is pleased and delights to bless those who worship Him. Even your spiritual strength is fortified in worship. When one is low, a spirit of worship guards their vitality, and encouragement returns from the sweetness of adoration.

Worship Through Sound / Music

Music is the most common and widely embraced expression of worship. Singing and musical worship awaken the heart of devotion. The Scriptures command us to lift our voices to the LORD:

"Let the message of Christ dwell among you richly as you teach and admonish one another with all wisdom through psalms, hymns, and songs from the Spirit, singing to God with gratitude in your hearts."— (Colossians 3:16, NIV)

"Singing psalms and hymns and spiritual songs among yourselves, and making music to the Lord in your hearts."— (Ephesians 5:19, NLT)

The psalms celebrate the diversity of instruments and the joyful sound of praise:

"Praise him with a blast of the ram's horn; praise him with the lyre and harp! Praise him with the tambourine and dancing; praise him with strings and

flutes! Praise him with a clash of cymbals; praise him with loud clanging cymbals. Let everything that breathes sing praises to the LORD! Praise the LORD!"— (Psalm 150:3–6, NLT)

"Sing your praise to the LORD with the harp, with the harp and melodious song, with trumpets and the sound of the ram's horn. Make a joyful symphony before the LORD, the King!"— (Psalm 98:5–6, NLT)

"Sing out your thanks to the LORD; sing praises to our God with a harp."— (Psalm 147:7, NLT)

In Scripture, the prophets often prophesied to the accompaniment of music, intertwining the prophetic spirit with instrumental worship. *(1 Samuel 10:5-6).* David is a profound example—he played his harp through seasons of joy and anguish, composing psalms and pouring out his soul before the LORD. His music soothed King Saul, driving away torment and ushering in divine peace. *(1 Samuel 16:23).*

Music is God's creation for worship. It elevates the spirit and enables ascent into higher realms. It attracts the presence of God—as when the Spirit came upon Saul among the company of prophetic musicians.

Never trivialize any grace within the body of Christ. Psalmists and instrumentalists are guardians of worship. Their gifts edify the Bride and open pathways for deeper encounters with God. Their labor strengthens the spiritual environment, enabling others to worship, serve, and grow more effectively.

Music heightens spiritual sensitivity, creating ideal conditions for the manifestation of spiritual gifts. This is why prophetic ministries as seen in the Scripture so often intersect with music—it softens the heart, opens vulnerability, and creates a channel through which the Spirit flows freely.

Take advantage of the graces in the body of Christ. Do not struggle alone in seasons when your fervour dwindles. Many have labored so that others may rise on the strength of their ministry. Their music, preaching, and service are vehicles of grace—freely given to aid your spiritual ascent.

The body of Christ was designed for interdependence:

"The human body has many parts, but the many parts make up one whole body. So it is with the body of Christ... But we have all been baptized into one body by one Spirit, and we all share the same Spirit. Yes, the body has many different parts, not just one part."— (1 Corinthians 12:12–14, NLT)

"If one part suffers, all the parts suffer with it, and if one part is honored, all the parts are glad. All of you together are Christ's body, and each of you is a part of it."— (1 Corinthians 12:26–27, NLT)

Worship Is Obedience

A heart truly yielded to God is an obedient heart—and an obedient heart is, by its very nature, a worshiping heart.

The LORD rebuked Jerusalem through Isaiah, exposing the danger of hollow, lip-deep worship: *"And so the LORD says, 'These people say they are mine. They honor me with their lips, but their hearts are far from me. And their worship of me is nothing but man-made rules learned by rote.'"*— (Isaiah 29:13, NLT)

This reveals the futility of external worship disconnected from obedience and relationship. *Acceptable worship requires a heart aligned with God.*

The prophet Samuel echoes this truth: *"... 'Does the LORD delight in burnt offerings and sacrifices as much as in obeying the LORD? To obey is better than sacrifice, and to heed is better than the fat of rams.'"*— (1 Samuel 15:22, NIV)

Obedience—responsive listening and surrender to God's will—surpasses ritual. **True worship is active, relational obedience—not mechanical performance.**

Worship Is Serving Purpose

Worship and service are inextricably linked. Jesus' declaration in the wilderness establishes this divine order:

"...You must worship the Lord your God and serve only him."— (Matthew 4:10, NLT)

This summons believers into exclusive devotion—adoring God and serving Him in alignment with His purpose. Worshipers are servants, and servants are worshipers; the two cannot be separated.

From the beginning, God designed humanity to live for His pleasure and glory. Worship is not merely an activity—it is the ultimate purpose of our existence. The psalmist captures this reality with joy:

"Worship the LORD with gladness. Come before Him, singing with joy. Acknowledge that the LORD is God! He made us, and we are His. We are His people, the sheep of His pasture."— (Psalm 100:2–3, NLT)

To worship with joyful acknowledgment is to live fully aware of our identity as His people—yielded to the Shepherd who made us and called us His own.

Isaiah echoes this eternal intention:

"Bring all who claim Me as their God, for I have made them for My glory. It was I who created them."— (Isaiah 43:7, NLT)

Humanity was created with inherent purpose: to reveal, reflect, and magnify the glory of God. We manifest this purpose through worship—adoration expressed through obedient living.

The apostle Paul completes this divine thread, tying worship directly to God's eternal plan: *"In Him we were also chosen, having been predestined according to the plan of Him who works out everything in conformity with the purpose of His will, in order that we, who were the first to put our hope in Christ, might be for the praise of His glory."*— (Ephesians 1:11–12, NIV)

To worship God rightly is to serve His divine intention—to fulfill the very purpose for which you were created. Your obedience, your assignment, your calling, your sacrifices, your daily walk—*all become expressions of worship,* bringing praise to His glory through every facet of your life.

Together, these truths unveil worship as a dynamic expression of a yielded, obedient heart fully engaged in the God-ordained purpose of glorifying Him—through both reverent devotion and faithful service. Worship is far more than ritual; it is the vibrant, obedient response that aligns every dimension of a believer's life with God's will and eternal design.

THEMES ON A HEART OF WORSHIP

Worship from a Heart of Love for God

The secret that sustains your love for God is often found in heartfelt meditation—reflecting on how far He has brought you, what He has rescued you from, the gospel, and the sacrifice of Christ: the blood He shed for you (*John 3:16*). Your personal reason for loving God—your salvation's foundation—may be tied to a profound purpose He has given you. For many, that divine purpose becomes an unshakable anchor.

As David wrote: *"The one thing I ask of the LORD—the thing I seek most—is to live in the house of the LORD all the days of my life, delighting in the LORD's perfections and meditating in His Temple."*— (Psalm 27:4, NLT)

Love for God fuels the desire to dwell continually in His presence.

God commands us:

"And you must love the LORD your God with all your heart, all your soul, and all your strength."— (Deuteronomy 6:5, NLT)

Echoing this, David confesses:

"For You do not desire sacrifice, or else I would give it; You do not delight in burnt offering. The sacrifices of God are a broken spirit, a broken and a contrite heart—These, O God, You will not despise."— (Psalm 51:16–17, NKJV)

True worship flows from a broken, loving heart—not merely outward acts.

Worship is a demonstration of love, actuated through obedience. While many are drawn to singing and music as expressions of worship, true worship begins deeper—within the heart. Ultimately:

"And now these three remain: faith, hope and love. But the greatest of these is love."— (1 Corinthians 13:13, NIV)

As long as genuine love remains—even in turmoil—worship can continue. Love, therefore, becomes the greatest generator of spiritual fervour.

Worship from a Steadfast Heart

Like Job, believers are called to steadfast worship—maintaining reverence and praise even in the midst of trials. Job's story stands as a testament to unwavering devotion despite immense suffering (see Job 1–2).

Scripture exhorts:

"Give thanks in all circumstances; for this is God's will for you in Christ Jesus."— (1 Thessalonians 5:18, NIV)

And again:

"Consider it pure joy, my brothers and sisters, whenever you face trials of many kinds, because you know that the testing of your faith produces perseverance. Let perseverance finish its work so that you may be mature and complete, not lacking anything."— (James 1:2–4, NIV)

Steadfastness in worship steadies the heart, anchoring it in God, and enabling spiritual growth and maturity through life's challenges.

Worship from a Heart of Gratitude

Gratitude is both a natural outcome and a powerful generator of spiritual fervour. It invites joyful worship and pleases God deeply.

"Since we are receiving a Kingdom that is unshakable, let us be thankful and please God by worshiping Him with holy fear and awe."— (Hebrews 12:28, NLT)

"Enter His gates with thanksgiving; go into His courts with praise. Give thanks to Him and praise His name."— (Psalm 100:4, NLT)

Paul instructs:

"And let the peace that comes from Christ rule in your hearts. For as members of one body you are called to live in peace. And always be thankful. Let the message about Christ, in all its richness, fill your lives. Teach and counsel each other with all the wisdom He gives. Sing psalms and hymns and spiritual songs to God with thankful hearts."— (Colossians 3:15–16, NLT)

Likewise: *"Always be joyful. Never stop praying. Be thankful in all circumstances, for this is God's will for you who belong to Christ Jesus."*— (1 Thessalonians 5:16–18, NLT)

And: *"Don't worry about anything; instead, pray about everything. Tell God what you need, and thank Him for all He has done."*— (Philippians 4:6, NLT)

Cultivating gratitude not only pleases God; it sustains worship, fueling spiritual fervour through every season and circumstance.

"The human spirit can endure a sick body, but who can bear a crushed spirit?"— (Proverbs 18:14, NLT)

Worship was designed to benefit the worshiper. In worshiping God, our souls are renewed, our strength is replenished, and like the eagles, we rise again. Our spirits are fortified to carry on serving God's purposes in and through our lives—with fresh fervour.

THE FIFTH GUARDIAN: CONTRITENESS—A Hunger and Thirst for Righteousness

JUDGEMENT

To be contrite in heart is to hunger and thirst for righteousness despite previous wrongs. It is to possess a heart soft and sensitive to the Spirit of God—ever watchful, ever careful not to grieve Him. This is ***contriteness of heart***: the soul-deep acknowledgement of your imperfections that stirs your inner man to seek God more, pursuing the perfection found only in Christ.

Contrition pierces the heart with conviction, creating a spirit tender and open to the Holy Spirit's work—yielded, responsive, and without resistance. It is a key guardian of spiritual fervour because it establishes the platform for true repentance and fuels the motivation to outshine the darkness of this fallen world. It empowers a heart of intercession for lost souls still bound in sin. A contrite heart is empathetic, knowing well that *you yourself were never righteous—nor could you ever be—apart from the gift of salvation.*

Thus, you stand in the gap. From this profundity of contrition flows the guardianship needed to preserve spiritual fervour.

"For thus says the High and Lofty One Who inhabits eternity, whose name is Holy: 'I dwell in the high and holy place, with him who has a contrite and humble spirit, to revive the spirit of the humble, and to revive the heart of the contrite ones.'" (Isaiah 57:15, **NKJV**)

"The sacrifices of God are a broken spirit, a broken and a contrite heart—these, O God, You will not despise." (Psalm 51:17, **NKJV**)

David was called a man after God's own heart because he **was** contrite in heart. Without contriteness, there can be no true humility—only self-righteousness.

A prayerless life reveals a lack of contriteness, for it betrays the belief that you can function without God. You do not make time for Him because you imagine you are fine either way. But if your heart were truly contrite, you would hunger and thirst for the perfection that only Christ can form within you, acknowledging your deep insufficiency without Him.

A Hunger and Thirst for the Word

This hunger for righteousness expresses itself as a deep longing for the Word—a sustained craving for divine truth that aligns the heart with the heartbeat of God. *"Blessed are those who hunger and thirst for righteousness, for they will be filled.*"(Matthew 5:6, NKJV) This is not a casual desire; it is a holy ache that refuses spiritual famine and presses into spiritual fullness.

This appetite must be cultivated deliberately and tenderly—small, consistent doses that enlarge spiritual capacity and inoculate the soul against apathy and lethargy. *"As newborn babes, desire the pure milk of the word, that you may grow thereby, if indeed you have tasted that the Lord is gracious."* (1 Peter 2:2–3, NKJV) Growth comes to those who feed, and feeding comes to those who desire.

Paul exhorts Timothy with apostolic urgency: *"But you, O man of God, flee these things and pursue righteousness, godliness, faith, love, patience, gentleness."* (1 Timothy 6:11, NKJV)This pursuit is not passive—it is a deliberate chase, a continual stretching of the soul toward God. Hunger sustains it. Thirst drives it.

The Bereans embody this posture with noble precision: *"Now the Berean Jews were of more noble character than those in Thessalonica, for they received the message with great eagerness and examined the Scriptures every day to see if what Paul said was true."* (Acts 17:11, NIV)Their eagerness was not emotional hype; it was disciplined devotion—the kind that tests, studies, confirms, and grows.

And righteousness has a force within it that refuses defeat. Even in failure, it compels movement. *"For a righteous man may fall seven times and rise again..."* (Proverbs 24:16, NKJV)Hunger gets him up. Thirst pulls him forward. The Word anchors his rising.

A Famine for God's Word

A famine is sweeping the earth—not of bread, not of water, but of the Word of the Living God. This famine is subtle, slow, and deadly, draining the vitality of nations and suffocating the spiritual life of multitudes. When men no longer treasure the voice of God, every other voice grows louder: culture, confusion, compromise, and carnality.

In such a time, the sons and daughters of God must become reservoirs—cisterns of truth deep enough to withstand droughts and overflowing enough to nourish the thirsty. This is the hour to anchor ourselves in the Word, for the times demand believers whose spirits are saturated with divine revelation.

Isaiah cries out with urgency: *"Seek the LORD while He may be found, call upon Him while He is near."* (Isaiah 55:6, NKJV). His words teach us that access to God's voice is a privilege, not an entitlement. Seasons of divine nearness do not last forever. The wicked must forsake their ways, the unrighteous their thoughts, for true seeking demands repentance—a turning of the heart and the mind. Yet to those who return, the LORD promises mercy and abundant pardon. In a world starving for truth, God offers Himself generously to those who hunger. *(Isaiah 55:1-3)*.

Psalm 32:6 exhorts: *"Therefore let all the godly pray to You while there is still time..."* (NLT). A contrite heart recognizes the urgency of spiritual timing. There are windows of grace that open and close—moments when God can be found more easily, when conviction is sharper, when His drawing is stronger. The wise pray while the window is open. The foolish delay until the soul dries beneath the famine.

And when the enemy rises like a flood, Isaiah 59:19 declares: *"The Spirit of the LORD will lift up a standard against him."* (NKJV). In days of famine, the flood of deception is fierce. But the Spirit Himself becomes our standard—lifting truth like a banner, resisting darkness with divine force, and strengthening those who stand in righteousness. A famine for the Word is a battlefield for the soul, and only those aligned with the Spirit withstand the tide.

Colossians teaches us to root deeply: *"Let your roots grow down into him… Then your faith will grow strong in the truth you were taught."* (Colossians 2:7, NLT). Shallow roots cannot survive spiritual famine. Only those who bury themselves in Christ—hidden, anchored, nourished by the depths of His wisdom—will remain fruitful. When the world dries up, deeply rooted believers overflow with thanksgiving instead of spiritual malnutrition.

Paul reminds Timothy that we are soldiers: *"No one engaged in warfare entangles himself with the affairs of this life…"* (2 Timothy 2:4, NKJV). In a time of famine, distractions are deadly. Entanglements dilute devotion and weaken resolve. Soldiers survive famine because they focus—single-minded, disciplined, unmoved by civilian concerns. Their sustenance is obedience to the Commander.

Isaiah 60 calls forth a prophetic vision: *"Arise, shine; for your light has come! And the glory of the LORD is risen upon you."* (NKJV). In the midst of famine, those who carry the Word become radiant. Darkness cannot extinguish them; scarcity cannot starve them; the glory resting upon them becomes nourishment for nations. God raises His people as beacons—feeding the hungry with truth and illuminating the path for wanderers.

Amos warns: *"I will send a famine... of hearing the words of the LORD."* (Amos 8:11–13, NIV). This prophecy reveals the tragedy of delayed hunger—people will search for the Word when it is too late, wandering from sea to sea without finding it. The wise cultivate appetite now. The foolish awaken only when there is nothing left to consume.

Righteousness, therefore, becomes more than a personal posture—it becomes a garment that clothes the believer for famine days. Revelation proclaims: *"The fine linen is the righteous acts of the saints."* (Revelation 19:8, NKJV). Righteousness is visible, tangible, lived out in justice and love. Job echoes this imagery: *"I put on righteousness, and it clothed me..."* (Job 29:14, NKJV). Righteousness is not merely possessed—it is worn. It shapes how we walk, speak, judge, and serve.

Isaiah affirms: *"The path of the righteous is level; O upright One, you make the way of the righteous smooth."* (Isaiah 26:7, NIV). God ensures that the righteous are not swallowed by famine but guided with clarity and stability. Their way is made smooth—not without challenge, but without ruin.

Hebrews takes us deeper, teaching that discipline yields *"the peaceable fruit of righteousness"* (Hebrews 12:11, NKJV). Famine purifies. It exposes what is weak and strengthens what is true. And as we endure, Hebrews 13 calls us to continually offer *"the sacrifice of praise"* and *"not forget to do good and to share."* (Hebrews 13:15–16, NKJV). In famine, worship and generosity become warfare. Praise fills what emptiness tries to drain.

James commands: *"Be doers of the word..."* (James 1:22–25, NKJV). Famine is not survived by hearing alone. Only obedience protects the soul. And he declares: *"Pure and undefiled religion...is this: to visit orphans and widows in their trouble, and to keep oneself unspotted from the world."* (James 1:27, NKJV). This is the intercessory fruit of contriteness.

Authentic righteousness expresses itself in compassion and consecration. James crowns the teaching with this promise: *"The fruit of righteousness is sown in peace by those who make peace."* (James 3:18, NKJV).Peacemakers become planters of righteousness—cultivating spiritual life even in barren lands.

Jesus seals it all with the anthem of a righteous kingdom: *"Blessed are the peacemakers, for they shall be called sons of God."* (Matthew 5:9, NKJV)

And finally, the Lord Himself gives the antidote to famine: *"But seek first the kingdom of God and His righteousness, and all these things shall be added to you."* (Matthew 6:33, NKJV). When righteousness is the priority, provision is the result. When the Word is the pursuit, famine loses its power.

THE SEAL OF RIGHTEOUSNESS AS SECURITY FROM DIVINE DESTRUCTION

God's relentless search for righteousness in the earth stands as a solemn reminder that righteousness is not merely moral uprightness—it is divine protection. It acts as a spiritual bulwark against judgment. The Lord lamented through Ezekiel: *"I looked for someone who might rebuild the wall of righteousness that guards the land. I searched for someone to stand in the gap in the wall so I wouldn't have to destroy the land, but I found no one."* (Ezekiel 22:30, NLT)

This divine plea reveals that righteousness functions as a protective wall—when present, it shields; when absent, destruction draws near.

In biblical theology, circumcision was never the source of righteousness but its sign and seal—the outward testimony of an inward faith already credited before God. Paul explains this clearly: *"And he received the sign of circumcision, a seal of the righteousness that he had by faith while he was still uncircumcised. So then, he is the father of all who believe but have not been circumcised, in order that righteousness might be credited to them."* (Romans 4:11, NIV)

Thus, righteousness precedes ritual. Faith precedes ceremony. What was physical in Abraham becomes spiritual in Christ, for in Him we undergo a circumcision not made with hands. *"In Him you were also circumcised with the circumcision made without hands, by putting off the body of the sins of the flesh, by the circumcision of Christ."* (Colossians 2:11, NKJV).

He clothes us in Himself: *"But put on the Lord Jesus Christ, and make no provision for the flesh, to fulfill its lusts."* (Romans 13:14, NKJV). Without His righteousness, humanity stands exposed to divine wrath.

The story of Moses further amplifies this holy principle. Moses was obedient in worship, steadfast in service, and unparalleled in humility—*"(Now the man Moses was very humble, more than all men who were on the face of the earth.)"* (Numbers 12:3, NKJV).

Yet despite these virtues, he faced divine wrath for failing to honor the seal of righteousness—circumcision—required in his dispensation for every household male among God's chosen people, by not circumcising his son. *(Genesis 17:12-14)*. Scripture recounts: *"At a lodging place on the way the LORD met Moses and was about to kill him. But Zipporah took a flint knife, cut off her son's foreskin and touched Moses' feet with it...So the LORD let him alone."* (Exodus 4:24–26, NIV). This moment underscores an eternal truth: unrighteousness attracts destruction, but righteousness preserves life.

David affirms this urgency: *"Therefore let all the godly pray to You while there is still time, that they may not drown in the floodwaters of judgment."* (Psalm 32:6, NLT)Righteousness is not optional; it is demanded—urgently and immediately.

God warned Cain of this same principle: *"If you do what is right, will you not be accepted? But if you do not do what is right, sin is crouching at your door; it desires to have you, but you must rule over it."* (Genesis 4:7, NIV). Paul echoes the consequence of refusing righteousness: *"For the wages of sin is death; but the gift of God is eternal life in Christ Jesus our Lord."* (Romans 6:23, KJV). Acceptance is tied to righteousness; death is tied to sin.

God rejects worship divorced from righteousness. *"To do righteousness and justice is more acceptable to the LORD than sacrifice."* (Proverbs 21:3, NKJV) Amos is even more severe: *"Away with the noise of your songs! I will not listen to the music of your harps. But let justice roll on like a river, righteousness like a never-failing stream!"* (Amos 5:23–24, NIV).

Paul reminds believers that righteousness comes through faith, not ceremony: *"Consider Abraham: 'He believed God, and it was credited to him as righteousness.' Understand, then, that those who believe are children of Abraham."* (Galatians 3:6–7, NIV). Without faith, righteousness becomes impossible, and without righteousness, our best efforts are defiled. *"But we are all like an unclean thing, and all our righteousnesses are like filthy rags..."* (Isaiah 64:6, NKJV).

Noah proves the principle: righteousness preserves. In a generation overflowing with wickedness, *"The LORD saw how great the wickedness of the human race had become... His heart was deeply troubled."* (Genesis 6:5–6, NIV). Yet Noah was spared because he was righteous in the eyes of God—his righteousness built his ark.

Jesus Himself warns that righteousness determines destiny: *"Not everyone who says to Me, 'Lord, Lord,' shall enter the kingdom of heaven, but he who does the will of My Father in heaven."* (Matthew 7:21–23, NKJV). Without righteousness we cannot inherit eternal life. Nor can we see God, for: *"Pursue peace with all people, and holiness, without which no one will see the Lord."* (Hebrews 12:14, NKJV).

Simon the sorcerer gives us a sobering picture of the unrighteous heart. Peter rebuked him sharply: *"'May your money perish with you... You have no part or share in this ministry, because your heart is not right before God.'"* (Acts 8:20–21, NIV). Heart posture determines spiritual inheritance.

Hebrews issues an even more severe warning: *"Dear friends, if we deliberately continue sinning after we have received knowledge of the truth, there is no longer any sacrifice that will cover these sins. There is only the terrible expectation of God's judgement and the raging fire that will consume His enemies."* (Hebrews 10:26-27, NLT)Intentional sin extinguishes fervour, silences worship, and quenches the flame of righteousness.

So, believers are commanded to put the sinful nature to death. *"For you died, and your life is now hidden with Christ in God... Put to death, therefore, whatever belongs to your earthly nature... Because of these, the wrath of God is coming."* (Colossians 3:3–6, NIV). Righteousness is not passive; it is warfare.

Scripture calls us to plant in righteousness: *"Plant the good seeds of righteousness, and you will harvest a crop of love. Plow up the hard ground of your hearts, for now is the time to seek the LORD, that He may come and shower righteousness upon you."* (Hosea 10:12, NLT).For *"In the way of righteousness there is life; along that path is immortality."* (Proverbs 12:28, NIV).

This path is steady and sure. *"The way of the just is uprightness; O Most Upright, You weigh the path of the just."* (Isaiah 26:7, NKJV). Discipline may wound for a moment, but it yields a harvest: *"Now no chastening seems joyful... nevertheless, afterward it yields the peaceable fruit of righteousness..."* (Hebrews 12:11–13, NKJV).

Isaiah seals it: *"The work of righteousness will be peace, and the effect of righteousness, quietness and assurance forever."* (Isaiah 32:17, NKJV)

"But seek first the kingdom of God and His righteousness, and all these things shall be added to you." (Matthew 6:33, NKJV).

Once contriteness is established within you as one of the guardians of spiritual fervour, it compels you to seek God's kingdom and righteousness. The seal of righteousness guards, preserves, secures, and sustains—indispensable to worship, vitality, and divine protection.

CONVICTION AS A GENERATOR OF CONTRITENESS

Man is inclined toward error; the sinful nature seeks expression whenever vigilance weakens. The enemy hunts for an open window—any fracture through which he may steal, kill, and destroy. Yet the hope of the believer lies in this truth: God does not condemn. *"There is therefore now no condemnation to those who are in Christ Jesus who do not walk according to the flesh, but according to the Spirit."* (Romans 8:1, NKJV). The Spirit convicts—never to shame, but to cleanse. His conviction births a longing for righteousness.

Paul embodied this reality. He never forgot his former life as a persecutor of the Church. That memory did not cripple him—it cultivated contrition. It preserved humility, fueled zeal, and generated unwavering spiritual fervour that produced unparalleled labour in the Great Commission. He confessed he had done more than the other apostles, yet declared himself the least because of his past. Conviction kept him burning.

Only those who realize the depth of their sin can appreciate the complete forgiveness that God offers them. This in turn creates a heart deeply broken in contriteness, that even humility abounds, and the inner drive to do more and more of the good work of God's righteous Kingdom.

This is the nature of holy conviction: it compels you to counter former darkness with present light. It is the internal insistence that what once lay broken must now be redeemed. Conviction refuses complacency. It generates fervour. It reignites zeal. It strengthens the guardians of spiritual vitality within you.

Conviction is the opposite of guilt. Guilt weakens, drains, and pushes the soul deeper into sin resulting in spiritual death. But conviction arrives with grace—empowering, lifting, cleansing, restoring. It equips the believer with the resources needed both to conquer sin and to rekindle spiritual passion.

The power of conviction that stirs up contriteness, which in turn keeps your spiritual fervour ablaze and your zeal for service constant, is the very force that drives you and keeps you clear of sin. Paul, speaking to the Corinthian church concerning a previous severe letter of rebuke, reflects on how it produced godly sorrow within them:

"Now I am glad I sent it, not because it hurt you, but because the pain caused you to repent and change your ways. It was the kind of sorrow God wants His people to have, so you were not harmed by us in any way. For the kind

of sorrow God wants us to experience leads us away from sin and results in salvation..." (2 Corinthians 7:8–10, NLT).

This conviction—here called sorrow—creates a holy pain in the inner man, steering you away from sin and generating the contriteness that guards spiritual fervour. It fuels the desire for purity, awakening a hunger and thirst for righteousness so that you may be filled. Paul continues,

"There's no regret for that kind of sorrow. But worldly sorrow, which lacks repentance, results in spiritual death. Just see what this godly sorrow produced in you! Such earnestness, such eagerness, such concern to clear yourselves, such indignation, such alarm, such longing to see me, such zeal, and such a readiness to punish wrong. You showed that you have done everything necessary to make things right." (2 Corinthians 7:10–11, NLT).

Here, conviction matured into contrite behaviour and produced zealous action—demonstrating renewed spiritual fervour and the resolve to do everything necessary to make things right. That is the result of the power of conviction.

Conviction keeps the five guardians alive. And as they operate, they sustain your zeal, establishing you as an unstoppable force set apart for the advancement of God's kingdom and the fulfilment of divine purpose.

THE FIVE GUARDIANS OF SPIRITUAL FERVOUR:

CONCLUSION

With these five guardians, you are shielded from spiritual lethargy. They are deeply, intricately connected; weakening one weakens all. A steadfast devotion to these guardians is essential for preserving spiritual vitality.

They feed into one another, strengthen one another, and create a divine circulatory system of fervour.

Once all are established within you, spiritual growth accelerates. Advancement through higher planes of maturity becomes continuous and unstoppable until you mature into the fullness of Christlikeness, to the glory of God.

With the five guardians of spiritual fervour, your spiritual maturity is kept growing and strong; therefore, the corruptions that often pursue servants of God—and seek to bring them low—are averted. Whether it is the love of money stalking believers called to steward great wealth for the glory of God, or the seduction of power shadowing those appointed to seats of governance, these guardians fortify you with the maturity needed to remain humble, steadfast, and anchored in the purpose of Christ.

They produce the brokenness that keeps you connected to God, reminding you of the possibility of a fall so that complacency never gains ground. They cultivate the heart that worships, adores, and fears the Lord. Without these five guardians, decay is imminent, corruption is inevitable, and the power you believe you wield will instead wield you—ushering in pride and destruction. Therefore, observe these guardians diligently; keep them alive as principles renewed continually, that you may remain in the favour of the Most High. For this revelation was given to preserve your purity, your strength, and your integrity in all your dealings.

With the five guardians of spiritual fervour at work in your life, spiritual growth and zeal for service become fluid progress, tangible strength is evident, for you now understand not only the direction of your life through the guardian of purpose, but the posture of your heart to carry it out and the spiritual maturity relevant for the right mindset to take the journey to become the fullness of what God ordained you to become with full assurance that the victory is yours, all glory to God.

The next prudent step to take is to understand the lifestyle discipline you ought to live by as a prudent Christian, and the hindrances to your divine progress which you ought to demolish from your life's path that you may experience this great freedom completely, as you walk in the grace of the revelation of the five guardians of spiritual fervour.

GENERATORS OF SPIRITUAL FERVOUR

E XPLANATIONS

<u>HOPE</u>

Hope is the confident expectation and anchor of the soul, providing stability and strength even in difficult times. It keeps the believer fixed on God's promises and future.

Hebrews 6:19 declares, *"This hope we have as an anchor of the soul, both sure and steadfast, and which enters the Presence behind the veil."* (NKJV)

This hope is not abstract—it is an anchor driven into the very Presence of God. It tethers your soul to a realm beyond fluctuation, beyond circumstance, beyond earthly instability. It is *sure*—unshaken by storms. It is *steadfast*—unyielding when the winds of delay or hardship blow. Hope drags the believer beyond the veil, into the eternal reliability of God's character.

Jeremiah 29:11 assures, *"For I know the thoughts that I think toward you, says the LORD, thoughts of peace and not of evil, to give you a future and a hope."* (NKJV)

Here God reveals His inner counsel—His intentions toward His people. His plans are not reactionary; they are rooted in divine benevolence. Hope flourishes when you understand that God's thoughts toward you are peaceful, constructive, and forward-moving. This verse injects confidence into weary hearts, reminding them that God's plans stretch beyond present pressures.

Isaiah 40:31 encourages, *"But those who wait on the LORD shall renew their strength; they shall mount up with wings like eagles, they shall run and not be weary, they shall walk and not faint."* (NKJV)

Hope here becomes transformative power. Waiting is not passive; it is an act of worshipful expectancy. As hope holds the gaze of the believer toward God, strength is renewed, vision is elevated, and the impossible becomes attainable. Hope makes the weary soar, run, and walk without collapse.

Romans 15:13 proclaims that joy and peace abound through trust in God, causing us to *"overflow with hope by the power of the Holy Spirit."* (NIV)Hope is not a human achievement—it is a Spirit-generated force. As faith rises, the Spirit fills the believer with joy and peace until hope overflows, spilling into thoughts, actions, and confessions. This hope becomes contagious, resilient, and unstoppable.

Psalm 42:11 urges, *"Hope in God; for I shall yet praise Him..."* (NKJV)Here, hope becomes warfare. The psalmist commands his own soul to place its confidence in God. Hope becomes the bridge between despair and praise, carrying the believer from heaviness into worship. It is the declaration that *praise is coming—even if my soul trembles now.*

Hope remains a vital thread alongside faith and love—though love is greatest *(1 Corinthians 13:13).*

<u>LOVE (AGAPE)</u>

Love is the enduring desire and commitment to others inspired by Christ's love for us. It sustains spiritual vitality and produces perseverance.

The English word *love* is profound yet limited in its capacity to fully communicate the depths intended in Scripture. The Greek, however, is richer for expounding on this context, presenting several layers of meaning that bring out distinct expressions of love.

The Greeks used multiple words to describe what we broadly call love: *philia* (brotherly love or affectionate friendship), *storgē* (familial affection), *eros* (romantic or passionate love), and *agapē* (divine, self-giving love). Among these, *agapē* stands as the highest and purest form—it is not rooted in emotion or attraction but in will, sacrifice, and covenantal commitment.

Agapē is the love with which God loves us—a love demonstrated supremely in Christ's sacrifice—and it is the love we are called to mirror in our relationship with others and with God Himself. This love flows from divine nature rather than human impulse.

It is the love that forgives when wronged, gives without expecting return, and endures through trial. When Christ commands us to love God with all our heart, soul, and strength *(Luke 10:27),* it is this *agapē* love He calls for—a love that consumes the entire being in devotion and obedience to God.

Hebrews 6:11 says, *"And we desire that each one of you show the same diligence to the full assurance of hope until the end."* (NKJV)

Love expresses itself through diligence. It does not waver or grow cold. It propels believers into consistency—into the *'full assurance'* of hope that lasts until the final breath. Here, love is not mere sentiment; it is stamina. It is the holy force that refuses retreat, the inner fidelity that continues long after emotion has ceased shouting.

This enduring quality of love—the perseverance that continues even through adversity—is a hallmark of agapē. It transcends emotion, anchoring the believer's actions in faithfulness. True love, therefore, becomes an engine for diligence; it keeps believers steadfast, faithful, and spiritually alert.

And Hebrews 6:12 exhorts, *"That you do not become sluggish, but imitate those who through faith and patience inherit the promises."* (NKJV)Love guards the believer from spiritual dullness. It drives imitation of the faithful, the patient, the steadfast—those who refused spiritual lethargy and pressed into inheritance. Agapē is active, never idle; it moves the heart to obedience and the hands to service. It awakens the spirit, stirs holy pursuit, and rebukes any slumber that would rob inheritance.

Paul prays in *Ephesians 3:17–19* that Christ's love roots, grounds, strengthens, and fills believers with the fullness of God through the revelation of its immeasurable depth. Here love is not sentimental—it is structural. It roots and grounds the believer, giving stability, identity, and capacity.

In Greek, Paul's focus again centers on agapē —a love that forms the foundation upon which spiritual life is built. It is both the soil in which faith grows and the structure that keeps believers upright amid storms. Love fortifies the spiritual frame, giving the believer an unshakeable center from which all power and obedience flow.

The apostle John reiterates, *"God is love, and he who abides in love abides in God, and God in him."* (1 John 4:16, NKJV)

Love becomes the environment where God Himself dwells in the human life. To walk in love is to walk in the very atmosphere of God. Here we glimpse the divine circle of agapē —originating from God, poured into our hearts through the Holy Spirit, and returning back to Him through our obedience and worship.

Love for God, therefore, is not merely emotional affection. It is the total offering of one's will, strength, and devotion to honor Him. This love transforms every area of life, bringing spiritual vitality and divine reflection.

Love is the flame that warms every other generator and nourishes spiritual vitality. It is the continual fire of agapē , feeding the soul, guarding faith, energizing hope, and making the believer a vessel through which the very nature of God's love flows.

FAITH

Faith: The Energy That Sustains Fervour

Faith is the power that sustains the believer through seasons of drought, delay, and unseen fulfilment.

"Now faith is the substance of things hoped for, the evidence of things not seen." (Hebrews 11:1, NKJV)This is not poetic language—it is divine architecture. Faith gives substance to what hope anticipates. It shapes the invisible into internal reality long before it manifests externally. Faith becomes evidence—legal proof—of things yet unseen.

Faith is the unseen force that anchors the heart when circumstances contradict promise, when feelings betray truth, and when progress appears invisible. Faith carries you into tomorrow when today tries to imprison you. *"For we live by faith, not by sight."* (2 Corinthians 5:7, NIV).

It is impossible to maintain spiritual fervour without faith, because fervour is forged in the fires of expectancy. Faith looks into the invisible and draws strength from the certainty of God's character. It is the lifeblood of endurance, the quiet roar within the spirit that refuses to yield, and the holy fuel that keeps the believer pressing forward into the fullness of God. Without faith, the inner flame flickers. With faith, it burns undiminished.

Hebrews 11 elevates Abraham as the model of faith—credited as righteousness because he believed God unwaveringly. Abraham's faith was not blind; it was obedient. He walked into uncertainty with certainty in God. His life testifies that faith transforms ordinary obedience into eternal impact.

Galatians 5:5–6 teaches, *"For we through the Spirit eagerly wait for the hope of righteousness by faith... faith working through love."* (NKJV)Faith is active. It waits earnestly, yet works through love. It holds expectation while expressing compassion. Faith is never idle; it is always partnering with the Spirit toward righteousness.

"And now abide faith, hope, love, these three; but the greatest of these is love." (1 Corinthians 13:13, NKJV)Hope stabilizes the inner man, fastening him to the promise of God; faith then gives that hope substance—flesh, weight, and reality. Hope gives faith its direction; faith gives hope its manifestation. Together they keep the believer moving, praying, and obeying with endurance, expectation, and joy.

Faith not only sustains; it strengthens. It expands a believer's capacity to believe God for more, to endure with resilience, and to remain spiritually aflame in the face of adversity. Faith is the internal engine that keeps the soul aligned with divine purpose, refusing to collapse under pressure or yield to spiritual fatigue.

Where there is faith, fervour thrives. Where faith grows, fervour rises. Where faith endures, fervour remains unquenchable.

GRATITUDE (THANKSGIVING)

Gratitude is the heartfelt recognition of God's goodness and provision, fueling continual worship and spiritual joy. Where gratitude flows, the heart of worship flourishes.

1 Thessalonians 5:18 commands, *"In everything give thanks; for this is the will of God in Christ Jesus for you."* (NKJV)This is not circumstantial thanksgiving—this is covenant thanksgiving. Gratitude is not dictated by environment; it is anchored in God's unchanging will.

Psalm 100:4–5 invites, *"Enter into His gates with thanksgiving, and into His courts with praise. Be thankful to Him, and bless His name."* (NKJV)Thanksgiving is the protocol of divine access. Gratitude ushers the believer into nearness, intimacy, and communion.

Philippians 4:6 encourages, *"Be anxious for nothing, but in everything by prayer and supplication, with thanksgiving, let your requests be made known to God"* (NKJV)Thanksgiving breaks anxiety's grip and shifts the heart from fear to faith.

Colossians 3:17 reminds, *"Whatever you do in word or deed, do all in the name of the Lord Jesus, giving thanks to God the Father through Him."* Thanksgiving becomes the fragrance of every action done in Christ.

Psalm 107:1 praises, *"Oh, give thanks to the LORD, for He is good! For His mercy endures forever."* (NKJV)Gratitude draws strength from the eternal constancy of God's goodness and mercy. Gratitude keeps the spirit tender, joyful, and aflame.

THE FEAR OF GOD

The fear of God is reverential awe and holy respect that inspires obedience, guarding the heart from pride, complacency, and spiritual dullness.

Speaking of the early church, Acts 9:31 shows, *"And walking in the fear of the Lord and in the comfort of the Holy Spirit, they were multiplied."* (NKJV)Here fear and comfort walk hand-in-hand. Reverence stabilizes the church; the Spirit strengthens and comforts it. The fear of God frees believers from all of life's anxieties and worries for it facilitates the realization that God is bigger than our present hardships.

Cornelius *(Acts 10)* carried fear of God before salvation—but fear alone cannot save. Only when the Spirit came upon him did reverence become transformation.

Spiritual growth requires both reverence *and* the Spirit's encouragement. Only when the fear of God is paired with the Spirit's counsel and comfort does it produce holy reverence that fuels sustained fervour, obedience, and fruitfulness.

This divine partnership empowered the early church—and it will anchor and elevate your spiritual fervour through every high and every low.

<u>JOY</u>

Happiness is fragile and fleeting, rising and falling with the tides of circumstance. But joy stands in holy contrast—deeper, stronger, and enduring. Joy is the quiet confidence of a soul anchored in Christ, the assured knowing that God loves you, sustains you, and remains with you through every valley and every victory. *"Rejoice in the Lord always. Again I will say, rejoice!"* (Philippians 4:4, NKJV).

This joy is not emotional fluff; it is a generator of spiritual fervour. It fuels the heart with worship, steadiness, and holy fire. Paul carried this divine generator within his spirit—an unbreakable joy that produced sustainable fervency. He learned to be content in every circumstance because his joy was rooted not in happenings but in Christ Himself.

Joy, being a fruit of the Holy Spirit, becomes a reservoir of strength. When it flows through your life, the ups and downs lose their power to destabilize you. With the joy of the Spirit within, you rise above obstacles, recover quickly from weariness, and remain replenished, focused, and fervent in your pursuit of God.

<u>CONVICTION</u>

Conviction is the holy opposite of guilt. Like guilt, it exposes sin, but unlike guilt, it strengthens, lifts, and encourages. It is the sacred tool of the Holy Spirit that softens the heart, makes it contrite, and prepares it to receive healing grace.

Through conviction, the Spirit functions as Counselor, Comforter, and Helper—lifting you back into purity of function. Conviction propels you into consecration, into pure service, into a place your heart longs to remain. It becomes the platform for a steadfast spirit.

Once conviction arises, the essential resources to conquer sin and rekindle spiritual vitality are already present.

*These seven generators—**hope, love, faith, gratitude, joy, the fear of God, and conviction**—are foundational sparks that reignite and sustain vibrant spiritual fervour. They empower believers to serve God faithfully in every season, even when the soul is heavy—upholding perseverance, purity, and a joyful heart anchored in God's purposes.*

LIFE WITH THE FIVE GUARDIANS OF SPIRITUAL FERVOUR

JUDGEMENT

With the five guardians of spiritual fervour at work in your life, spiritual growth and zeal for service become fluid progress—an unbroken flow of grace, strength, and divine momentum. Tangible strength becomes evident, for you now understand not only the direction of your life through the guardian of purpose, but also the posture of your heart required to carry it out. You walk in the spiritual maturity necessary for the right mindset as you journey toward becoming the fullness of what God ordained you to become, with full assurance that the victory is yours—*all glory to God*.

The next prudent step to take is to understand the lifestyle discipline you ought to live by as a prudent Christian, and the hindrances to your divine progress which you must demolish from your life's path. Only then will you experience this great freedom completely, as you walk in the grace of the revelation of the five guardians of spiritual fervour.

Weights That Hinder Divine Progress: Casting Off What Holds Us Back

The apostle exhorts the believer with a charge both sobering and empowering:

"Therefore, since we are surrounded by such a great cloud of witnesses, let us throw off everything that hinders and the sin that so easily entangles. And let us run with perseverance the race marked out for us." (Hebrews 12:1, NIV)

This is not merely an encouragement—it is divine strategy. We are encompassed by a great cloud of witnesses, the faithful ones whose lives became living scrolls of perseverance: From David in caves, Abraham with the promises of God, and Moses in wilderness discipline to Paul's great work with the early church.

Their testimonies speak, urging us to cast off every hindrance with decisiveness, to discard sin with violence, and to fix our eyes on Jesus—the Author who initiates our faith and the Perfecter who brings it to maturity. Their endurance demands ours. Their victories instruct ours. Their faith fuels ours.

We Have Seen the Five Guardians of Spiritual Fervour. We have also seen the generators of spiritual fervour.But it would be imprudent—spiritually negligent even—to advance without addressing the *weights* that suffocate that fire. For fervour does not die simply because passion fades; it dies because weights accumulate.

These weights do not announce themselves with noise. They creep. They cling. They wrap themselves around the soul until movement becomes laboured and spiritual strength drains in silence.

And so, we turn to the necessary work: identifying, uprooting, and overthrowing the weights that war against spiritual fervour.

Renewal of the Mind: The Foundation for Freedom

True spiritual progress begins in the unseen chambers of thought. *"Do not be conformed to this world, but be transformed by the renewing of your mind, that you may prove what is that good and acceptable and perfect will of God."* (NKJV)

Romans 12:2 is not a suggestion but a royal summons. The apostolic instruction is the gateway to discernment, clarity, and spiritual agility. Paul is not telling you to think positively—he is commanding metamorphosis. Renewal is transformation by truth. Without it, the mind becomes a breeding ground for deception, stagnation, and compromise.

A renewed mind identifies weights; an unrenewed mind normalizes them. Where the mind is untransformed, excuses feel justified, envy feels natural, ignorance feels harmless, hatred feels deserved, and poverty-consciousness feels humble. But these are not mere patterns—they are **weights**. They slow your movement, drain vitality, dim spiritual sight, and choke your hunger for God.

Transformation begins when light of the Word of God floods the inner chamber and exposes the weights that once hid in the shadows. Renewal turns blindspots into battlegrounds—and battlegrounds into victories.

Desires of the Flesh and Temptations: Weights to Overcome

The desires of the flesh act as heavy, dragging burdens. Temptations weave subtle cords around the heart, restricting motion until fervour becomes faint. Even the spiritually mature are not exempt from this war.

Christ Himself demonstrated the pathway to victory: reliance on the Spirit and unyielding adherence to the Word *(Matthew 4:1–11)*. In the wilderness, He did not debate with temptation; He dethroned it with Scripture. He did not trust human strength; He leaned into divine alignment.

His example declares with thunderous clarity: **temptation is not conquered by willpower—it is conquered by surrender to the Word of God.**

Therefore, the call echoes: *"If anyone desires to come after Me, let him deny himself, and take up his cross daily, and follow Me."* (Luke 9:23, NKJV). Self-denial is not misery; it is mastery. It is the breaking of fleshly appetite that positions the believer for spiritual ascendancy. Put off the flesh, and fervour rises. Feed the flesh, and fervour suffocates.

Unforgiveness: A Stumbling Block

Unforgiveness shackles the spirit. It clamps the soul into immobility, hindering communion with God and connection with others.

"For if you forgive men their trespasses, your heavenly Father will also forgive you. But if you do not forgive men their trespasses, neither will your Father forgive your trespasses." (Matthew 6:14–15, NKJV).

Forgiveness is not emotional preference—it is spiritual necessity. A grudge is not a wound; it is a weight. It distorts perspective, poisons affection, and anchors the heart to past injury, robbing fervour of oxygen.

Even **self-forgiveness** is required. Many believers suffocate spiritually not because of the sins they committed, but because of the self-condemnation they cling to. Releasing others frees your race; releasing yourself frees your soul.

Sin and Willful Indulgence: Entanglements That Bind

Deliberate sin and repeated indulgence form invisible chains.

"Do not let sin reign in your mortal body, that you should obey it in its lusts. And do not present your members as instruments of unrighteousness to sin, but present yourselves to God as being alive from the dead, and your members as instruments of righteousness to God. For sin shall not have dominion over you, for you are not under law but under grace." (Romans 6:12–14, NKJV).

Paul does not merely warn—he reveals sin's intention: to reign. To rule. To enslave. Sin does not seek visitation; it seeks dominion. If unchecked, it weaves entanglements that restrict spiritual motion until the believer becomes sluggish, dulled, and spiritually numb.

Confession must be consistent and repentance continual. Turning from sin is not an event—it is a rhythm. You cannot burn for God while bowing to what He died to deliver you from.

Negative Influences and Mindsets: Weights of the Mind

The mind is the battleground where fervour thrives or dies.

"He who walks with wise men will be wise, but the companion of fools will be destroyed." (Proverbs 13:20, NKJV). This is not moral advice—it is a spiritual law. Association shapes outcome. Company shapes clarity. Influence shapes appetite.

Your environment is either sharpening your spirit or dulling it. Exposure is discipleship. You become what consistently surrounds you. Choose companions and content that sharpen you toward God. Remain among the wrong ones, and spiritual fervour will bleed out silently.

The Importance of Integrity and Focus

Integrity fortifies the soul; without it, fervour collapses inward. Distractions, double-mindedness, and self-centered pursuits become weights that muddy focus and distort spiritual aim.

Paul's cry becomes our posture: *"Brethren, I do not count myself to have apprehended; but one thing I do, forgetting those things which are behind and reaching forward to those things which are ahead, I press toward the goal for the prize of the upward call of God in Christ Jesus."* (Philippians 3:13–14, NKJV).

Pressing requires focus. Focus requires integrity. Integrity anchors you in righteousness so that your pursuit remains pure, undivided, and unwavering. Where integrity breaks, fervour leaks.

The Impact of Negative Witnesses and Offenses

Offenses are hidden weights—small in appearance yet devastating in effect.

"Do not grumble against one another, brethren, lest you be condemned." (James 5:9, NKJV). Grumbling fractures unity. Offense starves spiritual vitality. Negative voices surround the spirit with invisible heaviness that clouds discernment and suppresses fire. Forgiveness and release are not emotional strategies—they are *spiritual weapons* to live above offense.

Additional Weights That Hinder:

- Pride

- Stubbornness

- Laziness

- Lack of prayer and reading of the word of God

- Presumptuous sins

- Sins of omission

- A lying tongue

- Self-doubt

- Anger *("for anger gives a foothold to the devil." Ephesians 4:27, NLT)*

These are not inconveniences—they are burdens that restrict spiritual fervour.

Among the greatest weights is **wrong company**. *As iron sharpens iron, so a man sharpens the countenance of his friend.* (Proverbs 27:17, NKJV)Iron sharpens iron—but dull iron destroys edge.

"Do not be deceived: "Evil company corrupts good habits."" (1 Corinthians 15:33, NKJV). If you remain among the wrong voices, sin will crouch at your door, clarity will fade, and spiritual vitality will die.

The Role of the Holy Spirit: Our Helper to Overcome

The Holy Spirit is the divine strength within—the Helper who empowers believers to cast off every hindrance and walk in liberty.

He convicts, guides, comforts, fortifies, exposes, uproots, and breathes holy fire upon weary souls. He breaks entanglements. He exposes weights. He empowers movement.

The Spirit is both wind and fire—lifting and purifying the believer for fervent service. Without Him, the race is impossible; with Him, the race becomes unstoppable.

By actively **identifying and casting off these hindrances, believers run their spiritual race with greater freedom, perseverance, and jo y**—guarding their spiritual fervour and fulfilling God's divine purpose.

The Divine Supply and the Call to Grow

2 Peter 1:3–9 (NIV)

"His divine power has given us everything we need for a godly life..."

Here, Peter unveils a profound kingdom truth: ***provision precedes pursuit.*** God does not call the believer into godliness and then leave them to scramble for strength. He equips before He requires. Everything needed for holy living—strength, wisdom, endurance, discernment, purity—has already been granted. The believer's task is not to strive for access, but to walk in what has been provided. Divine power sustains divine purpose.

"Through these He has given us His very great and precious promises, so that through them you may participate in the divine nature..."

The promises of God are not poetic sentiments; they are spiritual conduits. Through them, the believer steps into participation with God Himself—partaking in His nature, His character, His purity, His power. By these promises, we escape the corruption that floods the world through carnal desire. Every promise is an invitation into transformation, a doorway into divine likeness.

"Make every effort to add to your faith goodness; and to goodness, knowledge; and to knowledge, self-control; and to self-control, perseverance; and to perseverance, godliness; and to godliness, mutual affection; and to mutual affection, love." (2 Peter 1:5–7)

These are not virtues to admire from afar; they are spiritual graces to pursue with holy intensity. Faith is the foundation, but it must not remain alone. Goodness must enrich it. Knowledge must sharpen it. Self-control must discipline it. Perseverance must fortify it. Godliness must dignify it. Affection must warm it. Love must crown it. This is the ascending ladder of spiritual maturity—the deliberate building of a life that reflects Christ.

"For if you possess these qualities in increasing measure, they will keep you from being ineffective and unproductive in your knowledge of our Lord Jesus Christ." (2 Peter 1:8)

These graces are not ornamental—they are functional. Their growth ensures effectiveness, clarity, fruitfulness, and spiritual potency. A believer who cultivates these attributes does not stagnate; they advance, mature, and multiply impact. Spiritual fervour is preserved through continual growth.

"But whoever does not have them is nearsighted and blind, forgetting that they have been cleansed from their past sins." (2 Peter 1:9)

Neglect breeds blindness. When these graces are ignored, the believer becomes spiritually nearsighted—unable to see far, unable to discern purpose, unable to perceive calling. The tragedy of spiritual forgetfulness sets in: forgetting cleansing, forgetting identity, forgetting destiny. The absence of growth leads to the erosion of fervour.

Thus, Peter calls the believer into a deliberate pursuit—a building up of divine virtues that preserve effectiveness, clarity, and spiritual vitality. ***This is the heart of the five guardians of spiritual fervour.***

THE CHRISTIAN LIFE THAT HARBORS THE FIVE GUARDIANS OF SPIRITUAL FERVOUR:

THREE PRINCIPLES

To fully embrace and protect spiritual fervour in one's life, one must cultivate three foundational lifestyle principles—***integrity, discipline, and faith.*** These are the vessels that carry and nourish the *five guardians of spiritual fervour*: **purpose, humility, steadfastness, worship, and contriteness.** Without these three lifestyle pillars, the guardians stand weakened, and the inner flame becomes vulnerable to erosion.

These principles distinguish the wise from the foolish, the prepared from the unready—just as Christ illustrated in His parable of the ten virgins. Understanding and practicing these principles guard the sacred flame within, ensuring it never flickers, never diminishes, never dies, until His return.

Matthew 25:1–13 (NKJV)

The Parable of the Wise and Foolish Virgins

"Then the kingdom of heaven shall be likened to ten virgins who took their lamps and went out to meet the bridegroom. Now five of them were wise, and five were foolish. Those who were foolish took their lamps and took no oil with them, but the wise took oil in their vessels with their lamps..."

"...And at midnight a cry was heard: 'Behold, the bridegroom is coming; go out to meet him!'... And the foolish said to the wise, 'Give us some of your oil, for our lamps are going out.' But the wise answered, 'No... go rather to those who sell, and buy for yourselves.' And while they went to buy, the bridegroom came, and those who were ready went in with Him to the wedding; and the door was shut."

"Afterward the other virgins came also, saying, 'Lord, Lord, open to us!' But He answered, 'Assuredly, I say to you, I do not know you.' Watch therefore, for you know neither the day nor the hour in which the Son of Man is coming."

This parable becomes our prophetic mirror. Readiness is not accidental. Oil is never gathered casually. Vigilance is the mark of the wise, and negligence the ruin of the foolish.

1. Integrity: Authenticity in Every Season

Integrity is the seamless union between the inner man and the outer expression. It is wholeness of character—consistent whether in daylight or darkness, celebrated or unseen, applauded or forgotten. The five foolish virgins carried lamps but lacked oil; their beauty was outward, not inward. Their light sparkled in the day but collapsed in the midnight hour. They appeared prepared, but the truth betrayed them under pressure.

The wise virgins, however, possessed integrity. Their oil was not a performance—it was a practice. They cultivated inward substance long before the shout at midnight broke the silence. Their beauty was rooted in character, not in impression. They embodied Peter's counsel to Christian wives which also applies to us as the Bride of Christ when it comes to integrity:

"Do not let your adornment be merely outward—arranging the hair, wearing gold, or putting on fine apparel—rather let it be the hidden person of the heart, with the incorruptible beauty of a gentle and quiet spirit, which is very precious in the sight of God." (1 Peter 3:3-4, NKJV)

Integrity ensures your light does not falter. It stabilizes devotion. It preserves identity. It guarantees that who you appear to be is who you truly are—before God, before men, and before the unseen worlds. Integrity is the weight of gold beneath the shine of the lamp.

2. Discipline: Commitment Beyond Convenience

Discipline is the daily commitment to spiritual readiness. It is the continual tending of the flame, the refusal to let neglect steal tomorrow's oil. The foolish virgins recognized the need for oil—but procrastinated. They valued convenience more than preparedness, assumption more than devotion. Their downfall was not ignorance; it was indiscipline.

The wise virgins carried extra oil because discipline taught them foresight. They refused to gamble with their destiny. Their vigilance was not panic-driven; it was purpose-driven. They labored in silence so they could shine in crisis.

Scripture commands: *"...continue to work out your salvation with fear and trembling, for it is God who works in you to will and to act in order to fulfill His good purpose."* (Philippians 2:12–13, NIV).

Discipline is partnership with divine intention. It strengthens integrity and preserves focus. It ensures that your lamp remains steady through the long night of delay, adversity, and spiritual warfare. Where discipline thrives, fervour endures.

3. Faith: The Anticipation That Sustains Vigilance

Faith is the living anticipation that God's promises will surely manifest. The foolish virgins lacked faith in the Groom's timing; their negligence revealed their unbelief. Complacency is often the quiet child of unbelief.

But the wise virgins lived in expectation. Their faith fueled their preparation. Their trust gave them foresight. Their confidence in the Groom's return sustained their vigilance. They kept their lamps burning because they believed His words.

Peter exhorts: *"Therefore, my brothers and sisters, make every effort to confirm your calling and election. For if you do these things, you will never stumble, and you will receive a rich welcome into the eternal kingdom of our Lord and Savior Jesus Christ."* (2 Peter 1:10–11, NIV)

Faith anchors discipline. Faith reinforces integrity. Faith breathes life into fervour. It not only is a generator of spiritual fervour, but also a lifestyle pillar that must be established in your life. It is impossible to be spiritually fervent without faith; for fervour is the flame of expectation, and faith is the oil that keeps it burning.

Conclusion: The Dynamic Trio That Sustains the Flame

Integrity, discipline, and faith are the three pillars of a prudent Christian lifestyle that harbor the five guardians of spiritual fervour. They keep oil in the vessel, flame in the lamp, and readiness in the soul. They guard against drift, deception, distraction, and decline. These principles are not optional—they are essential. Without them, fervour collapses. With them, fervour becomes unquenchable.

Be wise, therefore. Be vigilant. Be steadfast. Nurture what God has placed in you with deliberate devotion and holy determination. Guard your flame. Keep your oil. Stand ready—always.

For this is the legacy of the wise, the strength of the burning, the heritage of those who refuse to dim.

'Après moi, la gloire!'

THE FIVE GUARDIANS OF SPIRITUAL FERVOUR

CLARION CALL

Guarding one's spiritual fervour from dying—and thus quenching the fire of the Holy Spirit—is a challenge to many. This is what makes the revelation of the Five Guardians of Spiritual Fervour such a vital message for the souls of believers. Yet no journey begins without *intentionality*. You must choose to awaken. You must choose to answer. You must choose to learn your life's purpose under the first guardian of spiritual fervour. And if you do not yet know the divine script of your life, then this clarion call is especially for you.

To have the strength and maturity required to remain steadfast is impossible without being rooted deeply in the river of the Holy Spirit—the One who comforts, counsels, strengthens, and upholds us through life's frequent adversities. You need Him to cultivate a heart of humility that is humble by God's divine standard, not human sentiment. The great cloud of witnesses, recorded by anointed servants under the Spirit's inspiration in Holy Scripture, stand as patterns of righteousness for us to imitate.

Only the Holy Spirit can break one's heart in contriteness through the power of conviction, ensuring you remain vigilant, alert, and aflame in service and fervour.

The Holy Spirit is *indispensable* in our dispensation—especially in these latter days of the world. The Church must rise, stand, and heed the clarion call of the Most High. We must embark on the journey to **become**. Without the Five Guardians of Spiritual Fervour, the capacity to withstand this journey's rigorous demands collapses into futility. And to imagine you can carry the Five Guardians without the Spirit of God is an even greater folly.

Furthermore, though *99% of biblical principles* operate without bias toward one's spiritual standing, the Five Guardians of Spiritual Fervour stand among the select *1%* that can only manifest fruitfully in those who are born of the Spirit. Only such ones can truly bear divine fruit in their lives.

Therefore, dear reader, this clarion call extends also to **salvation** and **realignment**—for any who have drifted from the path of righteousness. This step is not only appropriate, it is *necessary* for you to step into the life that embodies the Five Guardians of Spiritual Fervour.

THE PRAYER OF SURRENDER

Dear Jesus Christ,

I come before You as I am—weak in my humanity—yet choosing to put my trust in You, acknowledging my frailty and insufficiency. Dear Jesus, I come to confess my sins and ask for Your forgiveness. Let Your atoning grace cover me with Your mercy.

*I confess with my mouth and believe with my heart that You died for my sins, that I may be reconciled to the Father, and that by believing in You I receive eternal life in salvation and the hope of resurrection. Today, I lay down my life before You and confess that **I am born again. Amen.***

Now, with the gift of salvation comes the promise of the Holy Spirit—who enters your life as a divine deposit, guaranteeing the greatness to come. And now:

THE PRAYER OF LAUNCHING

Sweet Holy Spirit,

I come as a child of God the King. This is my royal request to You, O Divine Helper, sent to me by the gracious hand of our Lord Jesus Christ.

I understand the Five Guardians of Spiritual Fervour—the purpose that gives me direction, the humility that keeps me acceptable to the Father, the steadfastness needed to stand untainted in a fallen world, the heart of worship required to offer sacrifices pleasing unto God, and the broken and contrite heart that grants me access to His presence.

*I now ask You, O Holy Spirit, to **launch me** into a life that embodies the Five Guardians of Spiritual Fervour, and to empower the lifestyle principles of integrity, discipline, and faith-driven living that will sustain that flame, keep oil in my lamp, and maintain my watch.*

I ask this trusting and believing in the mighty Name of Jesus Christ. **Amen.**

THE BLESSING

"And now—*"The LORD bless you and keep you; The LORD make His face shine upon you, and be gracious to you; The LORD lift up His countenance upon you, and give you peace."* (Numbers 6:24–26, NKJV)

May your spiritual flame for Christ abound in zeal and never burn out, in Jesus' mighty Name!

For soon the King shall stretch forth His hand and say—*"Well done, good and faithful servant... Enter into the joy of your Lord."* (Matthew 25:23, NKJV)

SHALOM and MARANATHA.

CHRIST'S Faithful Vassal,

JEHU :')

About the author

Yeshua S. Jehu, authors the five-book *Shepherd's Pouch* series. Tailored for believers, it tackles power, financial stewardship, wealth-building, destiny fulfillment, spiritual development, and sexual purity—equipping you to stand strong in integrity, mature in truth for leadership, discipleship, relationships, and personal life.

The Five Guardians of Spiritual Fervour, the fourth installment of the series, unveils the divine architecture required to sustain spiritual vitality and preserve one's first love for Christ. Moving beyond formation into preservation, this volume reveals five foundational guardians that protect the believer from spiritual lethargy, familiarity, and decline.

Through revelatory insight and practical wisdom, it introduces a cohesive framework for maintaining zeal, purity, steadfastness, and depth of devotion—equipping readers to guard their flame, remain spiritually fervent, and walk consistently in the fullness of Christ with unwavering passion, discipline, and spiritual maturity.

Interconnected yet standalone, each volume ensures you grow fully equipped, lacking nothing.

Connect with the Author

Follow me on social media to stay updated:

Twitter/X: @Yeshua_S_Jehu

Instagram: @Yeshua_S_Jehu

LinkedIn: @Yeshua Jehu

Stay connected—discover new updates, behind-the-scenes stories, and keep the conversation going. Connect, share, and be part of the journey.

The Shepherd's Pouch: A Five-Book Vision for Biblical Dominion

The Shepherd's Pouch is the visionary name of this transformative five-book series, with *The Five Guardians of Spiritual Fervour* serving as the compelling fourth installment. This volume shifts the focus from formation to preservation—revealing that once identity is forged and purpose is awakened, spiritual vitality must be guarded to sustain what God has built.

It equips you with revelatory wisdom for maintaining zeal, purity, and unwavering devotion, unveiling the divine architecture that protects the believer from spiritual decline and keeps the fire of first love continually ablaze.

That profound progression continues through the entire five-book series, delivered with the same consistent excellence—interconnected as a cohesive series, yet individually complete, satisfying, and independent.

Book 1 opened the door to managing influence and power with purity and divine cunning. Book 2 unlocked the first pillar: Finances/Wealth. Book

3, established the indispensable process of identity, transformation, and growth. *The Five Guardians of Spiritual Fervour* now secures it all—preserving the flame, sustaining the zeal, and ensuring that what was built is never lost.

There are the three pillars of human society from which dominion over the earth becomes possible through God's divinely set principles—pillars upon which this entire series teaches passionately: **Sexuality, Religion/Spirituality,** and **Finances/Wealth.**

These are the roots of dominion, power, and influence, without which the church cannot wield transformative power for divine effect. Discover how these pillars are rooted in Scripture, first revealed in Genesis 1:28 as the eternal formula for power, as you journey through the entirety of this series.

Experience the *"fruitfulness"* of true spiritual life that pleases God and reshapes society; the divine *"multiplication"* born from the purity of sexuality, radiating righteous integrity across every avenue of life; the knowledge to build wealth that empowers you to *"subdue"* the earth and enact physical change with authority; and finally, the *"dominion"* that manifests as you master these three pillars through the wisdom and revelation of the Holy Spirit—applied with unshakable practicality.

"Then God blessed them, and God said to them, 'Be fruitful and multiply; fill the earth and subdue it; have dominion over the fish of the sea, over the birds of the air, and over every living thing that moves on the earth.'" (Genesis 1:28, NKJV)

Unlock the complete series and step into your divine authority. God bless you!

Also by Yeshua S. Jehu

THE SHEPHERD'S POUCH Series

Book 1: The 48 Laws of Power Biblically

Book 2: Money Biblically

Book 3: The Principle of Becoming

Book 4: The Five Guardians of Spiritual Fervour

Book 5: Purity Rises from Above

"Dare to complete the pouch? Interlock power, influence, purity, and spiritual vitality—unlock their divine interconnectivity. *Hope to see you in the next volume, fully armed.*" :')